Confessions of a C

by

Liam Thornton

Foreword

Any resemblance to any human beings, or animals or birds, whether still alive or no longer with us, is purely coincidental.

I hope that any foul language, or medical detail, does not repel you.

I have tried to avoid blasphemous language.

In one of my parishes, there was an ardent Christian, a chalice-bearer in the local Roman Catholic parish. He was diligently supervising some electrical works in our Church building. One day, he came up to me in Church, with a winningly genuine sense of indignation. At some mishap, one of his workers had sworn in Church, whilst doing his work : "Oh, Christ!". The devout supervisor told me that he had shouted back to him: "Stop fucking blaspheming inside this Church!"

If you, Dear Reader, feel any slight, I apologise. I do not intend to hurt. Could you let it be, please, like England and Australia men or women's cricketers having a drink together after a hard fought Test Match?

I hope that you will see it all, as in the first words of my favourite Easter hymn, with my taking the liberty of applying it to my mundane context:

"The strife is o'er, the battle done".

From Matthew's early child-hood writing-book:

"One day a dog stole a bone and he ran away with it until he came to a stream. As he was going over the bridge he looked down and saw another dog with a bigger bone. He snapped at it but dropped his own bone."

PART ONE:

A COVID CLERIC

Chapter One:
What to do on Christmas Eve?
(9.40 a.m. 2019 in the
Vicarage's kitchen)

Father Matthew had come to learn that it was best not to snap at other dogs' bones. The endeavours of Bishops' corridors, advisors' suddenly emerging as if from behind the curtains, were not to be for him.

Once, it had bothered him, if just a little. Matthew was only a very slightly disappointed Cleric, that is a member of the Church of England's Clergy. He had announced at seven years' old that he wanted to be Archbishop of Canterbury, albeit not World King.

As he had allowed a paunch to develop, he had grown into (he trusted) a not totally pastorally insensitive, mild but not bitter, sense of resignation.

Christmas Eve morning had arrived, at last. Everyone else was busy, and was going, indeed expected (and without doubt felt entitled) to have fun on this Merry Day.

As ever, Matthew had in due time written his Christmas cards. Vastly now fewer in number, the posted cards had gone off, maybe twenty to thirty. Bcc internet messaging meant that he had been able to cheat for a number of years.

When younger, Matthew had devoted space within Advent Retreats to writing and posting two, or so, hundred cards, nipping out from the Retreat House. He had never found Retreats easy. There was too much self-examination.

By Christmas Eve, Home Communions had been completed.

He had a second tomato juice, getting the amount of Worcester Sauce just right. The name of that sauce always reminded him of his College at Oxford. He had thought to himself then that he was going to have his Salad Days. Those days had been indeed mere salad to the Beef Bourguignon of the Bullingdon Boys.

He mused to himself that that second tomato juice went well with his Second Class Degree (even if it had been a "Good" one). Those novels in English Literature had been just too long.

His friend, Robert, had actually read all of them to the end. For Robert at least, it was not an academic Flag of Convenience. He had under-gone an interview for a First. On 'phoning their tutor as to the result, all that Robert could recall was "Just missed it!" The tutor hadn't meant to be dismissive, but it came over as "Fuck off! Good-bye!"

Matthew reminisced a lot. Usually, it helped.

At 9.40 a.m., he turned to "The Times". In the 1970s, his family had had delivered "The Times", "The Sun", and "The News of the World". Flicking through the 'paper, its' contents necessarily slight on Christmas Eve, Matthew smiled slightly to himself as he recalled a previous

2

Archbishop's comment that he always read "The News of the World" to find out what his Clergy were doing.

Matthew had nothing to do, until the Crib Service at 4.00 p.m. He reiterated to himself the mantras of Christmas: never have Carols that are less than thirty years' old; never say that Father Christmas is a phoney; keep it short.

The liturgical drama of Holy Week was as nothing compared to any potential Yule-tide eruptions of indignation.

The tradition of the fixed Festal Hymns had been violated.

Against a loose comment by an earnest young Curate, lengthy reasonings would be required of parents to try to prove the existence of Father Christmas.

Parishioners' fury would be uncontainable, if a verbose and protracted exposition (in the mid morning Service) of God's becoming a human being meant that Christmas Day Lunch's triumphant Joint had been rendered ruinously smouldering.

Anyway, it was like any other Christmas. There would be many more just the same.

Chapter Two:
Getting Ready for the Crib
Service (1.40 p.m. 2019)

Matthew had enjoyed watching clips that morning of "Carry on Cleo": they were silly, but comforting, amusements.

He had had too many Christmas chocolate biscuits: as ever, opened prematurely. Sternly, he had vowed to the bottle of Scotch that one small glass was enough- his will had prevailed. He'd enjoyed his pipe.

He knew that he had, festively, to be the happy Church Father at Christmas. Nothing but happiness was to radiate from his face. There was no one not to be smiled at, nor to say to: "Happy Christmas! "

He didn't really mind. He quite enjoyed it.

He chuckled for a moment, as he recalled a recent Clergy Christmas Party when a Clergyman had said in Mockney, nursing a glass of mulled wine on his distended stomach: " I 'ate Christmas".

It was time to go. He felt that he liked the people of the Church and Parish. The South Coast's after-noon bright cloud was starting to go grey, like Matthew's hair. Debates would be on. Crib Service- do we go, or, maybe just go next year? Anyway, aren't the children just a bit too old?

Matthew was half-way, from the Vicarage, to the Church when he missed a 'phone call.

This would be another good Christmas.

Matthew began to cough.

Chapter 3
Smoking

A pipe was precious to Matthew. He liked to have at least three on the go. Any one of them could be mis-laid at any time, and it was always good to have at least one of the three pipes' drying out.

It seemed easier to write a sermon having had a couple of bowls.

He had tried cigarettes (a good last resort still), once affecting at University a black cigarette holder.

Occasionally, he would quip that he had given up smoking. Yes, he had given it all up, (pause), but only because of a current chest complaint. In Lent, he would contend that every Sunday during Lent is not really of Lent. Every Sunday was a Feast of the Resurrection, of Easter: and thus, for him, a Feast of pipe fumes.

As often, others would chuckle benevolently.

Perhaps, whilst killing time over the news-paper, he had smoked a little too much. That was it. Nothing else. Reaching the Church door, he just hoped that he wouldn't cough up all over the children at the Crib Scene.

Chapter 4
The Crib Service (2.50 for 4.00 p.m.)

His first post, as a Curate (that is, a deputy Vicar), had been at a glorious South London Christian Shrine. Standing in the Sanctuary during "Schubert in G" at Midnight Mass had been exhilarating.

Matthew's first training Vicar had said to him wisely: "Always be prepared. Get everything set up in advance. It's no good for you, or any one else, if everyone's scurrying around a few minutes before-hand."

Everything was now ready for the Crib Service. Matthew didn't blame any one, but by half past three he was still alone. In the meanwhile, he had had a drag on the pipe, but out-side the   Church. He knew that smoke-alarms do tend to go off.

Twice in his time at that suburban Shrine, incense had caused the alarms to blast out during Mass. Failing to be prepared on both occasions, Matthew had neglected his curate's duty, before the Mass, of turning off the alarm. The London Fire Brigade had had to stride up the aisle mid-Service, in their own robes of office.

In the quiet, Matthew began to think about Christmasses past. He liked to think that, to him, memories weren't always ghosts; in his loneliness, they were sometimes guests.

Just after he left the Vicarage, the Bishop 'phoned.

Chapter 5
Father Christmas (3.40 p.m.)

In mufti, and with costume bag, Gerald slipped discreetly into the Cloak-room. As a Curate, Matthew's own Father Christmas had once been rumbled by four year olds: the glasses and watch had done it. "It's him! It's Father Matthew". Always take them off.

Father Christmas emerged in triumph; but still no one else had arrived. As benign as in his stage character, modestly he sat down at the back.

Matthew had come to the existence of Crib Services late. As a teenager, he had burnt the oil of Midnight Mass, serving with a thrill at the altar. He had marvelled at the improbabilities of a Cleric's preaching at 11.45 p.m., and also of his audience's being able to take in anything of it at all, as that final glass of mulled wine was, dozingly, being regretted.

It was said that one particular Vicar at that Church, with an early start on the Great Day, even had at 2.00 a.m. his family's Christmas Day break-fast, and then the opening of presents.

Later Matthew had come to learn of the Christingle, a candle-inserted orange given out to everyone, festooned with all manner of esoteric things. Yes, Christ was the Light of the World, but was it really necessary to risk childrens' hair and hands, and indeed the Church's floor?

A Crib Service, though? Until this parish, he had had images only of a few families gathered cosily around the manger. Now, clearly, it had become the high point of virtually any Cleric's Christmas.

Suddenly, the doors started to flap to and fro. Marginally, parents looked keener than children. A few

7

couples were barely speaking to each other. Some children's faces betrayed disappointment that the request list to the North Pole must have been lost in the post.

Matthew knew that this was one Service that he couldn't start on time.

And still they came.

Very good for the attendance Register, and the annual jousting at Clergy Chapter in January:

"Yes, packed out again- to the rafters!".

"Cheek by jowl, I tell you! Cheek by jowl!".

"Had to turn them away!".

Elsewhere, Matthew had known a Cleric whose accuracy in claiming every possible working expense had not been reflected in that of recording numbers in the Register. His Parish Administrator had been able to speak of barely anything else to any sympathetic visiting Cleric. A Crib Service was worth at least four hundred in the book. Might even get away with five hundred.

At 3.45 p.m., he repeated to himself the three mantras.

The Service went on to be judged a great success. No Carol caused frowns. Santa wasn't rumbled. Forty five minutes meant that Drinkies weren't delayed.

Heavy-footedly opening his front door at 6.30 p.m., Matthew wished he could just simply now go to bed for the night. Five hours remained until Midnight Mass. The Scotch would try to woo him. The tobacco pouch would become lighter.

He heard the beep of the answer-phone. Christmas Eve: what was the crisis? The Bishop wanted him to 'phone back urgently. There was no reply at the Palace. No reply three times in an hour. Matthew would not now be able to enjoy watching the annual Christmas Eve's ribbing of Des O'Connor by Morecambe and Wise.

Chapter 6
The Christmas Vigil
(7.30-10.00 p.m.)

Between attempted calls to the Bishop, Matthew pottered around, trying to distract himself. He made scrambled eggs. He looked over his sermon for Midnight Mass, yet again. Happily, it could be recycled, in even briefer form, on Christmas Day. At last, the 'phone went.

"Hello, it's the Bishop here, Matthew. Nothing to worry about. I can't go to Midnight Mass at St Wilfrid's tonight. The Service is off. Seems that the Vicar and half the Congregation have gone down with some sort of 'flu thing. Can I come to you?"

"Yes, of course, Father. It'll be lovely to see you".

He had only three hours in which to drum up support. Proverbially, Midnight Mass was these days more honoured in the breach rather than the observance.

He thought that, in this crisis, the right word was "triage". He'd have to triage more people to attend, asking the Wardens and (through them) the members of the Parochial Church Council to 'phone round the Congregation rapidly.

At least he wouldn't have a further Vigil of clock-watching.

Chapter 7
The Bishop arrives (11.00 p.m.)

All was ready.

Nervously, Matthew waited in the car-park's chill. Reassuringly, he heard the waves. The Tide always went out. The Tide always came in. There was Continuity.

A few Worshippers had already arrived. Matthew knew that the Bishop was generous enough of spirit not to mind their festive antlers. He sympathised with the Bishop, most of whose work seemed to involve clearing up the road after the Wee Donkey. There were some consolations for Matthew in his not succeeding in taking Purple.

Energetically for the late hour, the Bishop bounded out of his car. "Very good to see you, Matthew. Very good. Thank you so much."

"Will you preside and preach, Father?"

"Oh, you preach, Father."

At 11.45 p.m. Matthew began to preach his due eight minutes. In the candle light, many were enabled to rest their eyes. The sermon's final word, a customarily loud "Amen", served its' usual purpose. Most were then alert for the next part of the Mass.

The Three Line Whip had worked. Twenty had become thirty-five. There had been no unnoticed hitches. The Bishop had had an altar. Maybe, the worries of a Bishop had abated for a while. At least, he'd been saved from that 'flu.

Matthew had always loved the walk home after Midnight Mass. Pubs shut. House lights out. Silent Night.

In his kitchen, the bottle of Scotch winked at him. Why not? Only one dram would do no harm. After all, to be in bed by 2.30 a.m. would give him at least three hours' sleep.

Chapter 8
THE GREAT DAY

Matthew knew by 11.30, of the Glorious Morn, that he had achieved every Cleric's aim (the three mantras' aside): All I Want, For Christmas, is- not to Get 'Flu. He hadn't woken quite at the targeted 5.30. However, there had still been a chance to have a smoke, catching up online on the dull Christmas Day News.

Adrenalin helped. Could years of adrenalin make you ill?

Stepping out of the Vicarage, he had reminded himself that everyone on the pavement to Church ought to be greeted with a fully audible "Happy Christmas!" He'd been advised, puritanically, that "Merry Christmas!" was inappropriate for a vicar.

He had met no one. Where had they been, and what had they all been doing? He wouldn't mind one day a lie-in on a Christmas morning.

The Services at 8.00 and 10.00 a.m. had "gone well", as everyone had over generously agreed. Before the earlier Service, the light in the Church's precincts had been agreeably lugubrious. At the later hour, he had sensed a muted, but widespread, fear of the clock's over ticking. Turbo-charged drives would have to be made to relatives in far off shires by 1.00 p.m. Beasts had to be saved from being unseasonably barbecued. He met his target of finishing within 50 minutes.

Many times Matthew had done the Christmas Day Drive. Driving to his late parents' home in Shropshire had been cathartic. Once, or twice, he had driven through a West End that was empty. Had there been some sort of nuclear attack?

In relentless Warwickshire, he had once fallen asleep. For brief seconds, catter-pillars of sleep had drawn down his eye-lids.

Matthew liked sleep. In "Who's Who", he would have put it down as a Recreation. A time ago, Matthew had slept too well after an over-dose. There had been no dreams. No stirring. Obliteration.

After his parents had died, he had stopped travelling on Christmas Day. He had no brother or sister.

A few years later he'd met Sarah. Christmas Day was one of those days when, most particularly, he thought of her. He knew that he had treated Sarah very badly. He hoped that she was okay. Some memories were indeed not guests. Emotional exorcisms were far trickier than paranormal ones.

As ever for Matthew on Christmas Day, sausages and mint sauce went well.

Victorian ethics made for a Christmas Day Walk. He met no one. Affecting St Francis, he chatted that after-noon to the birds and horses. They could refuse to come to him, but at least they wouldn't answer back to him.

Tired by 6.00 p.m., Matthew returned. He took his blood pressure pill, and his statin. He went upstairs, snuggled under his duvet, thought regretfully of Sarah, and then, exhaustedly, fell asleep, like a bear in a canyon of marsh-mallows.

Happily, Boxing Day was going to be quiet.

Chapter 9
Waking up on Boxing Day
(8.45 a.m.)

"Shit!". He hoped that his Teddy Bears didn't mind the language. He'd forgotten that, on that day of the week, there was always a Service: now- in only seventy five minutes' time. "Shit! Fucking Hell!".

Hurriedly shaving, Matthew remembered shaving, in shock and so with no expletives, as the news had been breaking about Princess Diana. Distracted, he had cut himself, as he had tried to conjure up a new sermon. Then the altar frontal had had to be changed to purple, the Church's electronic Bell turned funereally to every twenty seconds, and his own and his people's shock and grief accommodated.

He remembered, though, other expletives of one Sunday when he had woken up at only 7.14 a.m. for an 8.00 a.m. start. He'd shaved. He couldn't remember whether he'd showered.

Two people came on Boxing Day: faithful people. He called into the shop for his "Times". The queue was a little bunched up, but it was after all mid-morning. Paying for his 'paper, some "Clan" pipe tobacco and matches, he couldn't help himself but say: "You're an M.P.!"

"Yes, I used to be."

Track suit had, at least for this vacation, replaced Saville Row suit.

Matthew had always admired this former Minister: a Christian man of solicitorly detail, dealing with arcane but important matters concerning far off places and shores. Matthew was delighted when he agreed to come to the

14

Vicarage for a cup of coffee. Matthew regretted having eaten all of the Christmas biscuits, and the fact that dog hair remained on the rug.

His welcome guest talked freely, innovatively, and loyally for half an hour. Such energy. Such fidelity to a Prime Minister who'd, it was said, sacked him. Thirty minutes was too short.

After his Right Honourable guest had left, Matthew glanced at the kitchen clock: Noon had been safely reached. He had a glass of Taylor's, nibbled on the stilton (parishioners were generous), flicked through the 'paper, and hoped that the vicar of St Wilfrid's and his people were getting better.

On the beach, he noticed that some people didn't seem to know whether still to say "Happy Christmas!"

The tide was coming in, as if invadingly. Spray flumed all over the walls of the bigger houses. He wondered what 2020 would hold. Would people still be banging on about Brexit? Such media storms were mere sea froth, though, surely?

Chapter 10
Dog-days

Matthew enjoyed being a dog in the days just after Christmas. There was warmth, shelter, food, drink, and an occasional stroll. On the street and beach, he noticed that some people had stopped now saying even "Hello!". Perhaps, they were visitors and thus unused to the local notion that not to do so was a sign of rudeness, and not of urban caution. Sometimes you could just about extract a half-smile and a subdued reply, a mussel from a recalcitrant shell.

Stroking others people's dogs on the beach, he missed his old Staffie, and his German Shepherd. The old Staffie had once nicked a whole barbecued pork chop from charitably unremonstrating picnickers on the beach.

The Alsatian had had to be put to sleep, when not ancient. He had slipped a disc in jumping a break-water at high speed. Matthew had been barely able to take the Services the following Sunday.

Avoiding any imputation of favouritism, he made sure that, as ever, he wrote all his thank you letters on the same day (28th December). He hoped that his messages were not too sugary. He recalled that Margaret Thatcher and Tony Blair had set great store on messages' being hand-written, and that his mother had struck an adult god-child's name off the List for neglecting that duty.

Dog days made, happily, for virtually no e-mails. Domestic commitments kept fingers away from key-pads, at least for a while. Perhaps, and rather disturbingly, key-board warriors became for a while domestic warriors.

Snoozing by 10.00 on New Year's Eve, he was content not to be sitting shoulder to shoulder in a stuffy pub, as the momentous Hour crawled closer.

"Bang!" "Bang!". Matthew could not be bothered to get up to have a look in the sky. He wished his teddy bears a Happy New Year.

Neither the following morning, nor subsequently, could he exercise himself enough to make a Resolution. His past Resolutions had usually been forgotten, once they had been ignored.

Time had come for the comforting ebb and flow of a new Church Year. Deanery Chapter, local Clergy's happily meeting together, was soon to come. You got good soup there.

Chapter 11
Deanery Chapter (mid January)

"Yes, packed out again- to the rafters!"
"Cheek by jowl, I tell you! Cheek by jowl!".
"Had to turn them away!".

The hostess' fish soup was excellent. The fifteen local Vicars and Curates formed a Chapter which was it seemed unparalledly without rancour. They were steered by a former barrister, and his deputy, a retired senior civil servant: with the tiniest necessary pieces of iron in their large velvet gloves.

After the soup, the custom was observed that business be discussed. In this Chapter, a serious matter would be raised, followed by a hilarious anecdote or joke, and usually a slightly grumpy aside, and then an answer found. Initially resisted in banter or mild grumble, a Diocesan idea would be faithfully accepted and, in due course, unfailingly applied.

Matthew was too shy to offer an anecdote or joke, keeping any grumpiness to himself, but he always enjoyed the spectacle. He wondered whether the extroverts were simply more able than others to deal with their own shyness. It seemed to him that a Cleric needed to be shy in order to listen and to observe.

(Editor's note: the Revd Richard Coles spoke about Clergy shyness on Radio 4's Saturday morning Show on 15th October 2022).

Looking ahead to 2020, various plans were laid, and commitments made. At the end, prayer was offered, especially for an Archdeacon who had, the Chapter was told, a severe respiratory problem.

Chapter 12
Snowdrops, but no soup

Matthew's spirits always sank in early Autumn. Winter, darkness, and Christmas beckoned. February gave him hope. Fingers frozen, he liked to see the snow-drops in the Church-yard. He was most alive during Holy Week and Easter: it was real religion. Oxtail stew.

It was a pity that that Archdeacon had had to retire on health grounds.

The story from China seemed a bit remote, even bizarre.

With Lent's having begun on 26th February, Clergy would no doubt start now to say, at private Lunch parties, as they balanced Prosecco on (after a tough winter) their now even larger stomachs: " I 'ate Lent".

In his Study, Matthew smirked to himself, as once again in Lent, he remembered the oft told tale of a Principal of a Theological College, who'd gone on to be an Archbishop.

"What, what, have you given up for Lent, dear boy?", he'd asked an Ordinand.

A particular physical vice had been the reply.

"Oh, oh, what a glorious Easter Sunday morning!"

The news increasingly mentioned China. Worshippers at a recent Baptism had told him of their delayed journey from northern Italy.

Matthew liked the end of February: even with this year's Leap Day, payday came sooner.

He started on his first Sermon for Holy Week. He was beginning these days to run out of ideas. A friend had once preached a Harvest sermon word for word, from ten years' previously. Faithfully still worshipping at that

Church, a parishioner had exclaimed: "Thank you, Father. Thank you. I'd never heard those ideas before."

There was some talk that Clergy Chapter, in early March, would be voluntary, and without even soup. Matthew decided nevertheless to go. There was indeed no soup, but only a few members kept within the safe confines of their vicarages. There wasn't the usual hearty laughter. Brows were a little furrowed.

Chapter 13
"Brave new world" ;
"Which is my better side?"

"Oh, wonder!
How many goodly creatures are there here!
How beauteous mankind is!
O brave new world, that has such people in it!"
(The Tempest: Act 5 verse 1 line 185)

The mobile went.
"Have you heard the news? Have you heard the news?!"
Matthew hadn't.
He'd been enjoying a cup of tea, in one of the Cathedral city's quieter cafes, after a pleasant browse around the Church book-shop.
His fellow local Cleric spoke about a so-called Lockdown. Churches were to be shut to all. Even Clergy were not to enter their own Churches. They'd be encouraged to ZOOM the Services from their Vicarages.
To Matthew, such closures in this new world sounded neither beauteous nor brave.
For a start, there'd be queues at make-up departments.
Hair-dressers and barbers would be taxed as to what to say to Cleric after Cleric, who'd trot into their salons. A Service-book was all that they needed for the week-end, surely?
Overwhelmed, dry cleaning workers would have to draw in breath sharply: "Can't get them back for a week, sorry, dear."
But, would any of those places be open?

This, though, was to be no ordinary Lent and Holy Week. There would be glitz. There would be glam.

Any video stars amongst the Clergy would no doubt like their face's better side to show; Zooming Mass to the masses, with Intercessions on the Internet.

Where would be the best place for filming in the Vicarage? Kitchen table? Living room? Make an unused room into a chapel? The kids could always share a room for the short while that this period would no doubt last.

Better start the Spring clean, and put out modishly reassuring religious ornaments (a pretty cross here; clay pots for candles there). Soothing music from an ethereal convent, or monastery, would set a tone. Mystically rising incense could even be indulged, with no fear of what a waspish Cleric had once described as "Protestant coughing".

Chapter 14
The Dinosaur dines

As far as Matthew could tell, his Bishop had made a unique decision. It was certainly a wise one. Clergy, in this Diocese at least, would be allowed to enter, and take Services, on their own in Church, possibly Zooming them. Matthew was used to being in Church on his own, for private prayer. He remembered an elderly Cleric who would acidly complain: "I wish that people would stop coming into my Church."

Hastily, Matthew wrote letters to everyone on the Church's membership list, posting, and, in some cases, hand delivering them, on an evening of driving rain. Years previously here, he'd abandoned umbrellas; too many had been wrecked by coastal squalls. He now thought of the Alsatian who had loved heavy rain, falling snow (jumping at the snow-flakes), and once a violent lightning storm. Long-haired, he had hated sultry days.

In his letter, Matthew tried to show empathy and to avoid being patronising. He invited people to join in prayer, at home or elsewhere, at the time of Services. He recalled to himself the maybe romantic tradition of the Parson's praying solitarily in Church for the people.

He thought that he might as well practise Zooming a Service. Just before ten o'clock the next morning, he carefully propped up his mobile 'phone on the altar. Getting ready for a Service was complicated enough, without having to beg a mobile to behave.

He liked to start Services on time. The mobile kept him waiting for two minutes. It just sat there on the altar, slightly morosely. Matthew felt straitjacketed by the camera. Movements of the body, and modulations of the

24

voice, might be too risky. "Can't see you! Can't hear you!" viewers might protest at home on a Sunday morning, as they switched over to the Andrew Marr Show, or went to get another bowl of corn-flakes.

Mass had been said. Matthew played over the tape. Goodness, it was boring. He thought that he was boring enough already.

Swallowing hard, he decided that in the next circular letter, he would 'fess up to not being a video star. He would not go Zoom live, either from the Church or Vicarage.

The dinosaur went home to have an early dinner. It was oxtail stew.

Chapter 15
The Rising Dawn

Holy Week and Easter could leave people stewing. Yes, there was the drama of the story, climaxing in the desolation of Good Friday, and the almost naive, yet genuine, joy of the empty tomb.

"Doesn't the Church-yard look pretty?";
"The children do love an Easter Egg Hunt there."

Stewing usually began on Palm Sunday. One voice might be: "Wasn't it lovely to have that donkey?" Another: "Did you see what that donkey did on the Church path?"

Stewing at Christmas was usually at the dashing of expectations: tradition's seemingly having been trashed. A thing of the mind and, to a degree, of the heart?

Easter stewing was possibly a thing of the soul. Perhaps, it was the Full Moon. Maybe it was the themes of betrayal and desertion, loyalty and friendship, pain and glory, death and life.

This Holy Week and Easter, the hermit Matthew had no one coming into, as that acerbic Cleric had put it, "his Church". Therefore, it was a stress free week.

He performed the Ceremonies pretty much in full. COVID meant that there could be no donkey on Palm Sunday, nor washing of feet on Maundy Thursday. However, on his own there could be both prostration at the start of the Good Friday Liturgy, and a greeting (abundant with Alleluias) of Easter's Rising Dawn.

Colours of altar frontals were changed throughout the week. The Church was bereft of colour and ornament on Good Friday. The dinosaur even managed to post some photographs of the week on Facebook.

Despite the hour, Matthew always loved walking to Church before Easter Day's Dawn Service, as the birds usually twittered, and, in some cases, squawked. What must those women have felt as they had brought their burial spices to the tomb at that hour?

The sun had shone throughout the week. Matthew could barely remember rain on Easter Day. This was a Season of hope: Christian hope of Freedom.

Chapter 16
Bravery and beauty

Politicians said that soon we'd all be free. Such, indeed, were words of comfort for the frightened, the isolated, the queuing, and the be-masked.

"Isn't everyone so nice to each other?"

Shielders' shopping bags were brought back full, and their prescriptions promptly collected. The NHS was clapped every Thursday evening for their perseverance and bravery: a thing of gratitude, but maybe also of suppressed fear. People let each other pass on pavements, and over stiles; sometimes there was almost an embarrassed mutual jig.

Birds sang. They perched. They flew in the blue skies of that Spring. Gone were the car fumes. Gone, too, were the white violating trails of those magnificent men and women in their flying machines. Did the birds, as they sat loftily, wonder whether those human beings had at last come to their senses?

Had the blue skies even been caused by man's turning hermit?

Fewer cars on the roads had given dogs, delightedly, a clearer run after cats, and, on a good day, birds.

At low tide, as if magically, a paddler could even see the little ones darting around.

Who seemed to mind, too much, that at least for a while, we weren't allowed to have parties? Socially distanced, streets were allowed to rejoice at the 75th anniversary of VE Day in early May, when the sun shone once more, but that was it.

Heavy heartedly, but sincerely and bravely, people came to accept shackles on their freedom to visit loved, and indeed dying, ones. Funerals were reduced to six people; Matthew conducted two of them.

There was apprehension, but also a sense that we were, as it was put, all in it together.

Matthew said prayers of thanksgiving alone in Church on that 75th anniversary. Through the weeks, he said Mass on his own, 'phoned people who might be lonely, and delivered a weekly letter. He invited, and received, items for those letters, their often recalling times of national trauma, such as the War. Through the letters, he devised a childrens' competition for an Easter card, a Bible quiz, and a quiz naming pictured birds. Some letters he posted. He liked delivering the others. He would meet people, and talk also to the animals and birds.

In this new era, there was a glimmer, maybe more than a glimmer, that people could be brave, and, in their hearts, beauteous. Perhaps, when the Lockdown ended in the Summer, there might be a chance of something like a brave new world.

PART TWO:

A MASONIC CLERIC

Chapter 1
Two horns

Delivering his circular letters, contentedly, in mid June 2020, Matthew was looking forward to the easing of national restrictions in a few weeks' time. Churches would be able to reopen. It wouldn't be quite yet the so-called old normal, but common sense had surely won.

There'd be distancing, sanitising, and no singing.The chalice would be drank by the priest alone. The instruction was to have a bare minimum of wine in it.

Sharing the chalice could be a physical night-mare. Before Matthew had become a "Rev", one training Vicar had warned him of a particular much loved lady, who, unless a firm grim were kept on the chalice, would drain the lot. Matthew had had at least one such occasion of having to fight the good fight with her. Poor lady.

To his immense relief, the shaking of hands, along with, in some instances, bear or gorilla hugs (an observance over dignified by the term "The Exchange of the Peace") would be transformed into a discrete wave from a distance. Matthew had always found the existing methods to be potentially unhygienic, or intrusive, or insincere.

Walking along, he thought how much he loved this month. June just galloped away. March and November yielded up each day reluctantly. June was promiscuously fast, reluctant only to cede her light.

Matthew felt good.

"Aren't you the local vicar?"

Matthew was pleased to stop on the pavement to have a chat. Always good to speak to a new face. In any case, the sun was strong, and he was, as ever, a little out of condition.

"Yes, I am. I don't think that we have met. Are you a resident, or a visitor?"

"I live just down the road. I wanted to have a word, please. I'm told that you are a Mason. A Freemason."

Matthew couldn't tell if he was being welcomed by a fellow Brother, or challenged.

Neutrally, he replied: "Yes, I am. I don't do much these days. Was it something that you wanted to talk about?"

"No, thank you. Just asking. Just checking. Bye then."

"Bye, bye. Enjoy the sunshine!"

Matthew now felt a little agitated, as he completed the delivery round. What had that man meant by "Just checking"?

He knew that some people saw Freemasons as corrupt, and even blasphemous. In particular, a Cleric who was Masonic could only but have two horns.

Chapter 2
Two letters

A few days' later, in early July, there were two letters in the post. The first that Matthew opened was a Summons to a Masonic meeting. It was a pity that, a clash with a meeting of the Parochial Church Council, meant he'd have yet again to miss seeing his Masonic Brethren. Still, it would save travel and dining fees.

The second, in a rather larger envelope, meant that Matthew's life would never be quite the same again. His heart fluttered as, at the top of the first page, he saw in bold capitals: "**Private and Confidential**".

It was from the Diocese's chief solicitor, the Registrar.

Once previously, he had received such a letter of formal Complaint; they came under the Clergy Discipline Measure. Having paid in cash, on Christmas Day, for the family to celebrate at the local restaurant, he had been accused of having snitched his wad of notes from the Christmas Collections. The Treasurer's Accounts had soon shot down that vulture, but not before Matthew had shot down first a fist full of Zopiclone sleeping pills. The Measure could do that to Clerics.

Previous to that Measure, it had been said to be close to impossible for a Cleric to be sacked in the Church of England. A hugely expensive and arcane procedure had existed, but those convicted needed, pretty much, to have slept with all of the married parishioners, raided all of the local banks, or kidnapped the Sovereign. Other transgressions had been dealt with by a private word, or a side-ways move, or even, with good luck, a promotion.

Straight after taking his over-dose, he'd had the wits to call an ambulance. All he could recall of arriving at the

Hospital, late that Sunday evening, was being made to stand upright. Apparently, it had been to prepare him for his coma in Intensive Care.

He read on. A Complaint had been made that Matthew had forsaken the Cross for the Square and Compasses. Purportedly, he'd spent so much time with his Masonic mates as to neglect his God- called ministry.

Immediately, memories of that night of near self-annihilation all but overwhelmed him. He swore. He smoked his pipe, which helped him to realise that it could only have been that "just checking" man.

It was time for a walk. He knew that, in distress, distractions on a walk can help. Once, one of his mother's dogs had bitten her on the hand, as she was cooking giblets. Weeks' previously, the dog had bitten Matthew's father dangerously near his wrist. Matthew had had to insist on taking the dog to the vet to be put to sleep. He still remembered the kind lady, whom he had met on that final walk, and, who, without realising the crisis, had talked of matters local.

Soon, he met Sosha, undoubtedly the gentlest Rottweiller in the world. According to her owners, Sosha's walks always took a long time. Everyone wanted to pet her. Her mouth, the saliva of her teeth, oozed goodness, unlike the fangs of some human beings. Matthew petted her, petting his bruised self.

(Sadly, the wonderful Sasha, my source, passed away on 3rd February 2023- it was always a pleasure to stroke her, and to chat to her).

Chapter 3
An Entered Apprentice Freemason

Matthew was a Lewis, that is a son of a Mason. He was the grand-son of two Masons, and the step-nephew of two others. One of his step uncles had been a Grand Officer.

To Matthew, Freemasonry had always been simply there: neither corrupt, nor blasphemous. Many of the men of his family's circle, and in local business and politics, were on the Square, but not seemingly for advantage. It was just the way it was. A couple of local Vicars were Masons; they didn't have horns.

He remembered his mother's telling him of her delight at giving the Reply to the Toast on Ladies' Night, his father's being Worshipful Master.

The regalia was exotic. There was mystery about the ritual. What was in that little manual book kept in his father's regalia case? Occasionally, and in a way almost thrillingly, Matthew would have a peek.

His mother said that Masons would always financially support each others' widows and orphans, and that also they gave a lot of money to charities beyond themselves.

There was an edge to those dark-suited men as they went off, attache cases of gorgeous regalia in hand, to their externally nondescript temples.

Matthew applied to join his father's Lodge in Shropshire at the earliest age possible, a shade over twenty one, and whilst still at university. He had to be interviewed by two "Heavies", who were most endearing.

Before his Initiation in 1980 as an Entered Apprentice Freemason, he had imagined dark interiors, with brethren gloomily sitting on benches. As the blind-fold was ceremonially taken off him during that ceremony, he came to see that he was in a place of light, exuberant regalia, fine ornamentation, and smiling faces.

He'd then been toasted at the meal, the Festive Board. There had been singing. There had been much banging on the table. There had been cigars.

At the end of that mild September's evening, he and his father, and two step uncles, had stepped out to the car. Matthew had made his first regular step in Freemasonry, and he sensed that he would enjoy it.

Chapter 4
Keep telling the bank the new address

Matthew's Second Class degree (even if a "Good" one) meant that he couldn't stay on to be a postgraduate. He had hoped to research possible Masonic references in the writings of Dryden, Pope, and Swift.

The swelling of his arrogant head was reversed by six months of unemployment, as the autumn of 1981 turned, in Shropshire, to a bitterly cold winter. He couldn't even pass the Civil Service exams. He tutored a boy for Maths. He continued his Masonic research. He walked the dog.

"There's a 'phone call for you, Matthew", his mother had to shout up the stairs, four days after Christmas. The man was very well spoken. He was the Head-master of one of the great Public Schools in north London. A Master had had a heart-attack. Could Matthew start teaching in three days' time? Matthew had been on Oxford's list of those willing to take on suddenly any teaching appointment.

Matthew's father drove him down to London the next day, setting off back in driving snow. Only later did Matthew come to appreciate his father's selflessness in doing so. Matthew's mind was on himself.

Matthew was to lodge with a Classics' Master, his wife, and young children. For break-fast, and usually in mid or late winter sunshine, there was always firm honey on toast, as each morning Matthew sipped his tea in anxiety at the day ahead. Matthew would come to wish that he'd made some effort to keep up with them: those kind and non judgemental adults and children.

He could just about manage English, but was only an inch ahead of his pupils as he taught Latin and Divinity.

In his first Lesson, in his naivety, he learnt the expression "half-mast", as a sixth former indicated to him his failure in dress code.

Some of the boys could be brutes. One evening, he tried to emulate his predecessor's ruse of telling a ghost story in the dark, only to notice a boy's smoking at the back of the class-room.

There was for weeks a vile smell in the class-room. The cleaners did their best, until Matthew discovered a bag of urine in a cup-board.

Still, his colleagues were uncritical, maybe over charitably so. They knew that he was a willing stop-gap. As a Cleric, Matthew would not always receive such forbearance.

As a happy dispensation to them, Masters lunched and dined away from the boys. There was a Mess chitty. A jovial future MP (Editor: sadly now late) would burble and chortle away. One Lunch, a huge figure came in, a former and moustachioed Rugby International, to join the teaching scrum.

There was laughter there, easing the pain of his own mess in the class-room.

Matthew even managed to join his Brethren once in the West End.

He was sure, that for many years, he would dine off having taught at that School, if only for a term, given his predecessor's recovery. Still, he had no permanent job, but at least he now had a summer term's appointment. Having previously replaced someone who'd had a heart attack, he was informed now with pride, by some of his pupils, that he was taking over from a man who'd had a nervous break-down.

In rural Shropshire, the place must have been bleak in all but this summer term. Matthew enjoyed the rich cakes of after- school Tea. He would walk by local meres, and through remote villages, mercifully forgetting the turmoil of the class-room.

The sheltered Matthew's experience was soon widened. He went to the other ancient University, to take a teaching qualification. It was usually damp. It seemed to be, but probably wasn't, cold in spirit. The trouble was that it simply wasn't Oxford.

His tutors always enjoyed their mid morning "coffee" at a local pub. No essays were required. Class-room discipline wasn't taught: the intrinsic interest of the subject would create the discipline. He valued his term's teaching practice, it's being the first time that he had entered the building of a Comprehensive school.

His eyes were opened, though, as he taught English to vast Classes. The range of books was meagre; their condition poor. There was, as yet, no National Curriculum. One morning, the children of one Class all suddenly left the room, as a nurse came in to order an inspection for lice. Sometimes, as he walked home there was a sickly smell, as of a Chippy with out of date fat. The

A final Ball in early June had led to Matthew's being dumped by his companion at about 2.00 a.m., or so, in favour of, as it was put, a Paraguayan diplomat.

The Ball's finished, Matthew , after table tennis at 7.00 a.m. (for those who had nothing else to do, or weren't entirely wrecked) and then a nap, had gone onto a mid morning stroll by the Cambridge waters with two or three other survivors of the Ball.

On the path-way, as they trudgingly walked, an unflagging member of those Pitcaigners (he'd performed on stage at the Ball, garland-receivingly) had burbled away, not to impress but generously to cheer up others, his being by turns Bill McLaren, Richie Benaud, and Peter O'Sullevan. For ever after, all swore that he'd been a very good take on Rory Bremner.

An appointment in the soft under belly of Oxfordshire awaited Matthew. It was permanent. He had lodgings, as a house tutor. He came to learn that 11 year olds can be more intellectually demanding than those hitting adulthood. One Class he never mastered. In the final Lesson of his first year, a water-bomb had drenched him. He did not take them on to O Level.

His sixth form Class was brilliant. At the end of his second (as it turned out final) year, three of them were awarded A Grades, probably despite Matthew's efforts. However, he rued, near the end of the final lesson with them one Saturday morning, his having shouted a pupil out of the room with "Piss Off!"

Two of his pupils had turned out to be Film Stars. One had been Tiggerish; the other mildly cynical. They had become adept at playing internal gloom.

It was a town of deep snow-drifts, and of summer heat that made after-noon Lessons far easier, as the boys slumbered on their desks. No interactive teaching then, happily.

Matthew even managed to join the Brethren of the School's Lodge, held on two balmy Summer Saturday after-noons, in the local and ornate Guild Hall. Masonry was good.

After a year, though, Matthew had begun, literally to wake up to think: I don't want to be doing this job anymore.

He wanted to do what he thought that the local Vicar did. Especially, he wanted to take the Services. Today, we would say that he had been inspired by that priest.

He had come to see that he had no future in School-mastering.It seemed to him that you had to have it in the blood. You needed to get a kick out of it. The Lesson last thing in the week had to be as important to you as the first one that you had ever taught. You had to relish reffing the games, as wind blew and rain spat in your face. You had to be keen to run the chess club, or to have soldiers bashing the square. All such pursuits were noble. They were not for him. Also, he couldn't face three decades, or more, of telling people to shut up.

Mind you, he enjoyed umpiring the cricket, which was always physically a little more difficult after Tea.

Matthew spoke to his local Vicar. He talked, too, to the School's Chaplain, a gentle man who, with his intelligence and humour, could contain the most barbarian Class of fourteen year olds in the last Lesson of the week.

The Chaplain wisely pointed out that Matthew saw only one tenth of a Vicar's work.

The Head-master was a Vicar's son, and an alumnus of a great Public School in the south. He had prolonged Dickensian side-whiskers. Graciously, he encouraged Matthew in his sense of vocation. He didn't hesitate to think that for himself it meant all the work of having to fill a vacancy.

Plucking roses as Matthew arrived, the Bishop took him into his curiously red painted study.

Matthew's path went on to be relatively smooth through selection Conference, and into a Theological College back in Oxford.

He left behind the stress of School- mastering. He could study God's Word. He could pop up to London to meet his Brethren.

Early in his first term at that Theological College (Anglo Catholics liked to style it a "Seminary"), one evening, he found in his pigeon-hole a paper drawing of a Masonic symbol. There seemed to be an antipathy in that place to Freemasons, and their Clerics' two horns.

Feeling intimidated, he feared a bang on his door that night. He deduced the perpetrators. He went next day to their daily Meeting. They saw themselves as the Old Guard, baggishly preserving the traditions. They admitted the symbol.They said that Matthew had been put forward to join a prestigious society of holy priests, but that his Masonic identity had been leaked to it.

Matthew pledged to remain neutral between their faction, papalists, and the other one of old fashioned Anglicans. He would keep his head down. However, twice a year he slipped out for an evening to London to meet his Brethren.

Two thirds' through his time at the College, the Church of England's General Synod declared that Freemasonry was not compatible with being a Christian. Such rendered a host of its' previous bishops as not Christians, including an Archbishop in the mid-century. Happily, the Report was referred not for action but discussion.

Thirty years' later, Matthew noted contentedly to himself that it was still being discussed, albeit with the occasional and maybe paranoid claim that the wondrous work of some new Vicar was being thwarted by a supposed local Masonic cabal.

He secured, in Theology, as previously in English, only a "Good" Second Class Degree (by those days, now called an Upper Second). He went on to be Ordained, first as a Deacon then as a Priest, to serve at the London Shrine. He came to know Masons there. He went to Lodge with them. They asked no favours. Being a Freemason would cause him no great grief for nearly three decades more. He went on to ministry in a New Town (as a Team Vicar, that is an upgraded Curate), and then to the sea-side, becoming there finally a fully fledged Vicar.

Then came that second letter.

Chapter 5
Thoughts of Dunblane

The letter's having arrived just after 9 a.m., Matthew had no proper time to ponder it by pipe. He had to go to School Worship at the Church Primary School. His mind was distracted and frayed. He recalled a Bishop's saying that, amidst the stresses of ministry, going into a School was rejuvenating: if only for a while, it was an exalting of spirits, a shooing away of the advancing Black Dog.

Matthew was always slightly nervous before Worship, worried that he'd get wrong either a Bible story or one from the tradition of the saints, or make a nice sounding comment that turned out to be heresy. Matthew knew that he was too unimaginative to give a Talk on a topic.

He clung to story, which he reckoned was the least likely way in which for him to be totally boring to children. Years after children had left the School, they would talk to him, sometimes with surprising affection, about those stories: large lads in local pubs; once girls, now mothers, asking for a Christening. It was one of the best parts of his ministry.

This time he was not in a Hall, but an Office, by ZOOM. He was addressing the 5 to 7 year olds, with whom, as always, he hammed up the story. Deploying, even by ZOOM, a lot of waving of arms, and raising of his voice, he told, seasonally in late June, the tale of the martyring of St Alban, at whose death, drips of his blood had, it was said, caused red roses to spring up, amidst the reported thunder and lightning. He'd been advised that children like melodrama, within limits, and that, with their thus being not too utterly bored, you could slip in a quick moral, or spiritual, point

42

Still ZOOM was not the same as it might have been on Assembly stage. There, overridingly, something usually seemed to impel him. At times, he used to blame the Holy Spirit.

As he chatted with the kind staff in Reception after-wards, he tried to put into the back of his mind the increasingly gnawing sense of anxiety caused by the second letter. He knew that Clergy sometimes had to hide their anguish. They had to drive from the funeral of a child to a Toddler Group's tea-party.

Once, in early after-noon, he had had to lead an Assembly, in the New Town, having only just seen the footage on television of the Dunblane Massacre. His mind had recoiled, in the Assembly Hall, as he couldn't but surmise to himself what it might have been like as the gunman had swept the corridors of Dunblane's School, massacring the innocents, young and old.

The staff then hadn't seem to have known of the massacre. Why should they have had? After all, they were working hard, without access to television. Matthew came to reflect that now, in an age of social media, they'd have known even before he had walked through the main door. He had decided not to tell them.

Now, decades' later, getting into his car, he put on the seat-belt, with weary worry. He could secure his belt, but maybe not his future. Much pondering by pipe was needed.

Chapter 6
BBC World Service

Sleeping for Matthew was always difficult after any Meeting of a Parochial Church Council. Had he said the wrong thing, or cut someone short, in danger of causing mortal offence?

It took hours of thought (and of his best intentioned but lazy prayers) to get ready for a Meeting of the Church Council. In the hours before any such Meeting, he would stride around the Vicarage, or stand in the shower, rehearsing his speeches and answers.

It was mid July, a Church's you'd imagine time of due midsummer slumbers. However, as ever at that time of year, the question anxiously remained: what are we doing for Harvest? This year, what about COVID?

In the rural Churches at Harvest, the point was obvious. God had given the growth, and the labourers had ploughed the fields and scattered. Why not band together thanksgivingly to God, at Supper, with tankards of cider, and song?

Elsewhere, for Harvest, it sometimes took a few months to confect a theme. As this year's debate inevitably drifted on, the Church Hall's barometer gauge remained stuffily at 78F. Matthew just wanted to go home, to spend two hours' puffingly ruminating, and then go to sleep.

Expectedly, those who early in the Meeting had called for it to be especially brief on " this balmy evening" (when, as they said, people simply wanted to be with their dogs on the beach, or with their loved ones at a late barbecue) seemed, sadly, by their long windedness not to have a dog to walk, nor loved one to go home to for a barbecue burger. Above their masks, the eyes of other members glazed over.

After a debate's lasting seemingly longer than those on the Holy and Divided Trinity in the early Councils of God's Holy Church, it was as if white smoke had signified that a cause for Harvest had been found: the local Air Ambulance. COVID meant that there could be no bashing into the sky of cider tankards at a Supper, but, still, who knew whose own injured body might not need to be lifted up and taken away to a far away hospital? Matthew knew, but didn't say, that the Masons gave much money to them.

Back home, he found that his baccy, as he affectionately and thus self-excusingly called it, had run out. He noticed that there was a missed 'phone call, his not recognising the number. There was no Scotch to wink at him. In the small hours, BBC World Service seemed again to Matthew to be one of the greatest things that the British could offer. Dry, friendly voices told you, in those dark hours, of scrapes afar, where once the Pith Helmets of our empire had not been knocked off.

Matthew knew that he would not sleep easily. The night was muggy. His thoughts were conflicted.

Yes, Harvest had been at last sorted out. He knew that he'd not stolen that money for a Christmas lunch. What was wrong with being a Freemason? Why had he hit Sarah?

Hazily through the night Matthew listened as the World Service mentioned even more infections and deaths. His blow to Sarah once again hit him.

Chapter 7
Study Day and being Well Oiled

Matthew had only but the highest admiration for the many other Clerics who liked to announce at Chapter that they always had a monthly Study Day away from the Vicarage, the inside of a week annually and separately for both Reading and also a Retreat, with at least one sabbatical already under their belt.

They managed so to order their parochial ministry as to be able to leave behind, for a while, the well oiled machinery of their Parish's life gently chugging away. Of course, they were not going off to be well oiled themselves.

They seemed pretty nifty at finding grants.

A Study Day was now required for Matthew, though, urgently and today. He postponed a dental check-up. What was wrong, anyway, with his teeth? They didn't hurt. He could always blame his pipe for their discoloration and crookedness. He'd save some money, too.

A potentially awkward pastoral visit could be delayed. On voice-mail, someone describing himself as a "concerned parishioner", had 'phoned the previous after-noon, wanting to speak to him. Matthew had been too busy preparing for the Church Council to reply. 'Phoning back now, to ask for a delay, he started to recognise the voice.

"Just checking" said that he apologised for, but did not say that he would withdraw, his letter to the Bishop. His Christian heart made him want to cease, but his Christian conscience meant that he could do no other. Slightly bitterly, Matthew pondered briefly the words of his mother (a Church-warden of twenty two years): "There are no people worse than Christians".

He recalled, too, that Clerics are paid not to answer back. Such was said to be part of their Calling. Prudently, it avoided fortune's trapping another hostage.

"I am really sorry to have made the Complaint, but I couldn't do any thing else. I tried to 'phone you yesterday before the Meeting of the Church Council, just in case you wanted to share anything with them. I know a couple of your Council- good Christians."

"Oh, thank you so much, for sharing it with me", Matthew replied with (he hoped a disguised) saccharine. Dead-battingly, he added: "I'll take it on board".

The Study Day, at home, began. Reading the documents of accusation, he could see that the sincere Complainant had as required a due interest, as a resident of the Parish. The Complaint could go forward.

It was asserted that Matthew went to Lodge at least twice and maybe three times' a week. Those blasphemous and nefarious activities had him shutting the Vicarage's door at Noon, only for him to reopen it, somewhat incompetently, at Midnight.

It was thought that, scandalously, he used to go to metropolitan flesh-pots. He would drink, or (as it is customarily termed in such a Complaint "consume") alcohol on those days of debauchery. It was strange, Matthew thought to himself, that no one, on his door-steps at his supposed Midnight return, had ever stood there with an alcometer or camera.

Matthew went to the corner-shop to get more baccy. As he walked, it was healing, as ever, to chat with dog-walkers and their dogs.

Puffing in his study, Matthew worked, if a touch ruthlessly, on some of the standard lines of defence:

(1)   Rubbish the Complainant - but, he didn't know anything about "Just Checking".

(2) Allege Collusion with existing malcontents- but, knowing nothing of his assailant, how could he determine potential contacts, crabs in the sea-weed?

(3) By evidence, refute the charges.

Years' previously, he'd read in another Parish's newsletter, the Wardens, as Praetorian Guards, saying that much of a priest's work is private and hidden. Seemingly, that priest's devotion to the Flock had been challenged there, too.

Being a priest was not a job. At risk of seeming high-minded, Matthew used to jest that he had given up having a job when he had ended School-teaching in the 1980s. It was a Calling. Clergy weren't paid. Having instead a stipend, they were given enough money so that they didn't have to get a job. They were Office-holders. Prosaically, for tax purposes, they were deemed to be self-employed.

The beauty of being a Cleric was that, by and large, you ordered your own day. Matthew recoiled from the thought of maybe in retirement (needing a top up) having to clock in and out at work. In that sense, his was an easy, even spoilt, way of life.

Given the duties of regular Services, and of Baptisms, Weddings and Funerals, along with School Assemblies, and Church or School Meetings, other time was free and potentially creative.

He might have liked every early after-noon to watch "Neighbours", "Doctors", or "Father Brown", and sometimes snoozily did so, but he knew that it was good to gird up the loins, and stretch the imagination: "Whom shall I visit this after-noon?" No one need to know whom he had visited, nor why. It was private and hidden. It was a privacy and hiddenness that it seemed people rightly both wanted and expected. It didn't necessarily swell pew numbers and church coffers, but a seed might have been sown. As with School, it was a demanding and yet golden part of ministry.

As politicians would put it, he really didn't want to give a running commentary on his daily doings.

Puffing again, and over a cup of mid-morning coffee, he received a 'phone call from the Archdeacon, who was, although unusually for him at this earlyish time of day not already well oiled, still characteristically oily.

Chapter 8

"Ah, Matthew"

A 'phone call from an Archdeacon (a Bishop's trouble-shooter) was almost always these days a very bad sign indeed. Once, Archdeacons would call by 'phone, or even at the Vicarage's door, in order to advise, encourage or console, to offer help with the Church's leaking roof, or a little personal assistance to a Cleric from the Discretionary Fund. Now, they had vultures circling above even them. There was this financial goal to be met, or that Mission target to be achieved. Archdeacons were judged by the perceived successes of their Parishes.

"Ah, Matthew", the 59 year old Archdeacon began. He had always seemed to be only 59, and thus years from a retirement as much anticipated by himself as by his clergy.

He was a charmer and a chancer, with his once lovely rural accent's now only occasionally slipping through his acquired Parsonical voice. He was a climber and a schemer, with a combustible temper. However, he toed the Diocese's line, and also, and even more importantly, knew which cupboards contained what skeletons, especially those of his fellow highly positioned Clerics.

"Ah, Matthew", he repeated, it seemed a little nervously. How was it (*whatever "it" was*) all going in the Lockdown? What adjustments had Matthew had had to make? What new initiatives was Matthew planning for when all was back to normal? How was the family coping with it all? Was he able to get away from the Parish, even if only briefly and COVID safely?

Matthew was sure that he could hear the clink of a glass.

He knew, too, that the Archdeacon couldn't mention to Matthew the Complaint (sub judice), even though, probably, he would have signed it off.

The Archdeacon was fishing. He was angling. A loose comment by Matthew, or a sign of stress, would have him hooked and then netted. Was this really a fishing for a man's soul?

Hastily reminding himself that no Cleric ever shows a chink, Matthew at once resorted to cliche. There never could be such a contented Cleric. He was so grateful for the 'phone call, and ended by hoping that the Archdeacon's dog was well. Sounding mildly disappointed, the Archdeacon rang off, assuring Matthew that he was in his thoughts and prayers.

Given the frequency with which the Archdeacon gave that assurance to his many Clergy, Matthew wondered how this thinking and praying elevated Cleric ever had time to get out of his chapel.

Relieved, Matthew puffed his pipe.He noted that the clock had just signified after-noon. On this Study Day, no visits or Meetings beckoned. No car journeys would need to be made. He poured himself a glass of sherry.

Anglo Catholic tradition insisted that the sherry be both very dry and very chilled. A well working 'fridge was essential. At Theological College, giving or attending a sherry party (always set at 5.45 p.m.) was a sign of being in God's Kingdom. The bell for 6.30 p.m. Evensong would start five minutes before-hand, such being the signal for one final slug, especially if it were a Thursday and, so, Guest Night.

Each Ordinand would have to lead the singing at the College's Evensong for a whole week some time in their two or three years' there. One petrified Ordinand had canvassed advice, which universally was to have a sherry immediately beforehand. It was said that he'd downed half a bottle with minutes to spare before his debut evening. His first line had dropped flat at once, and a voice had cried out in Chapel: "Roger's pissed!" It was thought that he'd gone on to be a bishop, apparently overseas.

Comfort would lie, too, for Matthew now in bacon butties: at least two of them. Sipping the very dry sherry, and munching his salty sandwiches, he found refuge, as often, in an old edition of "Yes, Prime Minister". He could even laugh mildly as the artifice of the civil servants reminded him of the slippery artistry of the Archdeacon.

For a while, comforted, he snoozed through "Doctors". He even managed to miss the murder at the start of "Father Brown". What was the point, then, in bothering to watch the rest of it? The Study Day had to be resumed, in any case, and, so, coffee had to be drunk.

As the kettle steamed, the door-bell rang. Matthew's time of introspection had been interrupted. He steamed, too, if only a little. He knew that his duty was to open the door, and not to hide away from the caller, like a debtor from a bailiff. After all, St Benedict had said that every visitor ought to be treated as if he, or she, were Christ.

On the door-step was "Just Checking", whom Matthew, sarcastically if fleetingly reflected, did appear to consider himself to be Christ. Using the autopilot of a Cleric's necessary and trained civility, he warmly welcomed him in: "Oh, it is good to see you. Do come in".

The Vicarage's path was muddy; there had been heavy mid summer showers. Christ didn't have time to wipe clean his shoes on the mat. His silent determination suggested that he intended quite soon to wipe Matthew on the carpet.

Chapter 9
"Shall we just pray?"

The custom of chilling sherry meant, happily, that no bottle could be seen as Matthew took Christ past the kitchen's open door. Matthew had managed, too, on going to the front door to remember to put the glass in the sink. He noticed that Christ's eyes slid side-ways as they went past the kitchen into the Study. Matthew knew never to keep any of his Masonic books and regalia in the latter.

"Would you like a cup of coffee or tea?"

"No, thank you. Can't stay long."

"Damn", Matthew thought. There was no time to leave his guest, and so to master his thoughts whilst making a cup. He suspected that Christ would stay long.

"How are you, Matthew?" Matthew hated being called by his first name, unless by family or friends. At School, it had been, until sixth form, surnames only. He had noticed that these days young men, from whatever type of school, often liked to call each other by surname.

He had a rule of equality. If writing to, or 'phoning someone, he would always refer to himself as "Father Matthew", however important the other person might be deemed (by self or others) to be in the life of the Church. The exception was fellow Clerics, and their families. However, he wouldn't upbraid any one if, familiarly, they addressed him as mere "Matthew". That was another hostage not to surrender to fortune. "Oh, he's terribly pompous. Told me off!"

Matthew said that he was fine. No chink.

"Matthew, I just want you to know that all this is nothing personal. I've prayed about it. I've prayed about you a lot. Yes, I am concerned for the Parish, but I am

53

even more concerned for you. I'm a Christian worried about you, a Christian. The Holy Spirit told me to help you, to save your soul."

As the man talked on not with brevity, it emerged that he was the Leader of some House Church Fellowship which he, guided only by the Bible and the Holy Spirit, had invented.

Matthew was somewhat sickened by the man's piety. He had always worked on the principle that a Cleric never comments on the state of someone else's soul, or indeed marriage, unless earnestly asked to by that person (and that person alone), and only then with great circumspection, and with as much compassion as possible. To his mind, here was someone who had made his points to a third party, the Diocese, and with neither care nor compassion.

He couldn't help but start to scorn a man who claimed, too, to be able to analyse and then judge as to whether a Cleric was neglecting duties. He wouldn't presume to tell a surgeon, a teacher, a plumber, a shop worker, or a parent how to fulfil their role.

Matthew knew that he had to guard his own words. Such was the only way to survive. Such was, too, part of trying in some small measure to be true to Christian principle.

Matthew went for stalling. He would stymie this apparently self-proclaimed fisher and saviour of souls.

"I can see that you have every good intention, but I really cannot discuss it with you at all, as I'm sorry you're the one who's made the Complaint ".

"Well, I'm sorry, too, that you feel this way. I just wanted to share it all with you. Are you sure?"

"Yes, thank you", Matthew replied now tight-lippedly.

"Shall we just then pray?"

For people like "Just Checking", everything seemed to be "Just". Seemingly, an inner implacable conviction was thereby disguised by a veneer of politeness. In particular, the term "Just Praying" seemed to be an insult to the Almighty, with the value of praying's being reduced to a bit like:"Just going to the shop for the 'paper".

"Just Praying" usually meant a rambling attempt to bend God's ear and so the divine Will, often interpolating opinion and gossip. Fifteen minutes only and you were lucky.

To Matthew, such praying was a coercing of God: the longer you prayed, and the more eye-screwingly hard, the more likely you were to get the result that you wanted. The arrow would eventually pierce Him.

For Matthew, praying for others was for human beings to sensitise themselves to the needs of others, taking the praying person (for at least a while) beyond his or her own desires for self. As a consequence, such praying would then, maybe, prompt him or her actually to do something good. For instance, at Harvest a prayer for the starving might prompt people to make larger donations, if within their means, in the retiring Collection for those starving in Africa. To Matthew, such self sensitisation and prompting to action was a working of the Holy Spirit, as human beings changed and grew.

"The Just Praying" did indeed last about a quarter of an hour. His guest luxuriated. He enjoyed himself, as he expatiated on the state, as he saw it, of Matthew's soul, and also on the alleged suffering of the Parish. He mixed sentimentality with a lecture to God, who needed to be told (and, it seemed, repeatedly so) about all that had happened and all that needed now to happen.

After a few minutes, Matthew stopped listening. His mind was on what to write as his Response to this vexatious Complainer. As his stomach rumbled, he remembered that he hadn't taken out from the freezer the chicken bits for tonight's casserole.

Christ left. He had indeed stayed long. He seemed pleased with himself. He said that he would continue to just pray for Matthew. Matthew hoped that there wouldn't be a Second Coming.

Chapter 10
Sand-castles

The first half of early August was always a Cleric's dream. Unless having family, the canny Cleric knew not to go on holiday at that time- to leave the sand bucket for a trip to Barbados in January, or at least Bognor Regis in late September.

Parish life was quiet. There was a perceived heroism in Father's "soldiering on", in the heat, whilst others paddled.

This year the local beach was more than usually crowded. COVID meant no mosquito bites abroad. Rather, people came for the day from south London, to be bitten here. Some locals whetted their lips each morning in keen anticipation of telling those Vikings to take their "bloody" ships from off the private roads. Letters could be written high-dudgeonly to the local newspaper. Dogs salivated to have just one chance at visitors' heels; the detritus of picnics made, too, for their scavenging diversions on twilight walks.

Matthew felt isolated. No Princes of the Clergy were around to be consulted. They were either at worthy Christian summer camps (perhaps secreting bottles in their suit-cases), or ministering to Ibiza's most needy Clubs.

Before break-fast, he often paddled in the usually already warm water. He would splash the water playfully and yet disconsolately. He would think of France over the horizon. He would think of John Stonehouse and Reggie Perrin's disappearing tricks. He would think, too, of suicides off this beach of which he had been told, and of Hamlet's "consummation devoutly to be wished". Such ultimate self-harm was trying once again to seduce him, a priest in God's Church.

Once this priest had hoped to build grand sand-castles. Now the turrets of his admittedly modest sand-castle had been kicked off. The water of the incoming tide was starting to flood its trenches.

He would walk home heavily, chin a little close to breast. The shop-keeper at the local shop would as ever be cheery, as Matthew bought his daily "Times", and weekly baccy.

Why did the sky have to be so fucking blue?

Matthew even tried failingly to re-learn Biblical Hebrew. Such might help his preaching. But, would there be any more preaching?

He had been told by his training Vicar to have one main point in a sermon. The Preacher ought to be able to sum up the sermon in one short sentence immediately beforehand. Those tucking into the Joint that Sunday lunch-time ought not to be reduced to saying: "Well he started with a joke, told us a story of when he was on holiday, but then rather lost me." The sermon ought to be about what the preacher believed rather than disbelieved. Any jokes ought to be clean, and, if at anyone's expense, that only of the preacher. Unless the preacher were Billy Graham, eight to twelve minutes was quite enough.

Angrily one day, as he strode home from the beach, Father Matthew vowed to preach a snorter that following Sunday, one about false accusations. Calmed by his pipe in his Study, he remembered that, with such tirades, usually the intended victim wasn't there. Otherwise, he or she would noddingly thank and congratulate the preacher on the Church door-step after-wards: "I'll glad that you told that lot. High time, too."

No, he would preach that Love was all. The trouble was that, for some Christians, as the sanctimonious code went, in destroying other people's sand-castles, they did so only in "Christian love and truth". The truth had to be spoken in love.

Chapter 11
A Kindly Figure from the Past

In the New Town, the then Archdeacon had been kindly. He was a large and energetic figure. He was an advisor, encourager and consoler. He could spot and sort out a leaking roof. His final words, on his visit, would usually be a gentle inquiry as to whether the Cleric needed any help from the Fund. Matthew had liked him.

On one occasion, coming to examine the silver-ware and Registers, as regularly required at any Church, he had asked to go into the Toddlers' Club. He had wandered around avuncularly, almost a cosy Father Christmas figure in Clerical garb. He had left the Hall, purring: "Splendid, Matthew. Splendid. Lovely to see the little ones playing, and the mums' chatting together." Here was a true fisher of souls. His previous ministry, in a large Evangelical parish, had delicately caught many souls for God.

"Ah, Matthew. Do come in. Do come in! It's lovely to see you, despite it all. How was the journey?" Matthew felt embraced by this man's Christian Love.

"Oh, very good thank you. It's good to meet up again, despite everything."

Every Respondee to an official Complaint had the right to Confidential support. The Bishop would suggest a name, and the Respondee could refuse, asking for another. Matthew, though, was delighted to be offered the support of this now retired Archdeacon. Matthew was led through to the book-lined study. There a photograph of a young cricketer, fine of figure, and raffishly wearing a cravat. "Put on a bit of weight since then", the Archdeacon pleasingly smirked, as he not too guiltily patted his girth. "Too much 'More tea, vicar', no doubt", he sniggered.

It was just past twelve. "Wait a minute, Matthew, just wait, please."

His host returned with a large glass of very well chilled dry sherry.

As they sipped, they discussed cricket, and how COVID was such a shocker. The Archdeacon knew that Matthew liked cricket. He had the elephantine memory of an Archdeacon, using it benignly. The Archdeacon said that he was so pleased that retirement had meant for him, at least pre-COVID, more time watching at Hove or Southampton. "Before then, too many Meetings in the after-noon!"

Matthew let the Archdeacon bring up the dreaded subject.

"Well, I'm not a Freemason myself. Never really had the time. Anyway, we Evangelicals, like you Anglo-Catholics, are meant to be against it, aren't we? Knew a few Freemasons in my last Parish, and some of the chaps in the Diocese were into it all: seemed decent types. That Archbishop of York in the 1980s described it all as a 'harmless eccentricity', didn't he?"

Freemasons had been pleased at that description by such a senior Bishop. Yes, there was much more to it than innocuous playing around, yet they had settled for such generous tolerance. Hitler had persecuted Freemasons. An intolerance towards Freemasonry was sometimes indicative of a wider lust for power and control.

"Yes", Matthew replied, "Anglo Catholics are meant to be against it". He told him of the symbol in his pigeon-hole at the Theological College, and then of his family's roots. He spoke of Bishops of the Diocese who had been Freemasons. The Archdeacon's face was momentarily inscrutable, as if he had not been totally unaware of that episcopal seal of approval. Matthew added that the Queen's father (amongst numerous other previous Kings and thus Supreme Governors of the Church of England) had been a Freemason. The Queen's cousin, the Duke of Kent, had been Grand Master since the 1960s. If it was good enough for Bishops and the Royal Family, it was good enough for him.

"I don't go to Lodge all that often, maybe once a month". Matthew knew a few Clerics who happily and weekly consecrated hours to whacking golf-balls, perhaps venting their fury.

Pouring a second and, to Matthew, another welcome glass of sherry, as a good Archdeacon, he came firmly and yet politely to the point: "Ah, dear Matthew, but what are you going to do?"

"Well, I suppose that I'll say that I see no clash with my faith. Many good Christians have been Masons. It doesn't take up much of my time. I'd never put it before attending a Church Meeting."

The Archdeacon's face became inscrutable again. It was as if he didn't doubt Matthew's sincerity, and might even have seen some truth in Matthew's self-justifications, but maybe he knew that it wasn't going to be all that easy. Did he know of other Clergy who like Matthew had been deemed to have over-stepped the mark? What had happened to them?

Matthew trusted, though, that the kindly retired Archdeacon would keep to his bond of confidentiality. He couldn't advocate for Matthew, but nor would he betray him.

The elderly man walked with Matthew to his car. From force of habit, he gave Matthew three ten pound notes: "Go on. Take it. It's from me, not the Fund- any way, don't have one now I'm retired! Treat yourself to a day out, watching the cricket, once they open the gates to us again. Don't know when that will be, though." Welling up slightly at this deed of compassion, Matthew shook the Archdeacon's hand warmly. He feared that others had already measured out their bags of thirty pieces of silver.

As he drove off, he turned back to wave at this benevolent priest, whose smiling face was that of a loving parent saying good-bye (with an inner sadness and worry) to a child about to embark on a long and maybe difficult venture in life. Did he suspect that Matthew's journey of life could only become even more bumpy? Matthew narrowly missed a pot-hole as he reached the end of the Archdeacon's drive.

Chapter 12
"Good heavens, if it isn't Matt."

Could there be a finer cricket setting in the world? Here a Duke allowed cricket lovers into his back garden. Cows mooed and chewed. They didn't seem worried that a hefty shot might hit them. Up in the Downs, you could even see the plains to a sea tranquil, at least from this distance.

Matthew had felt marginally more tranquil after seeing the gentle old Archdeacon, yet a knot remained in his stomach. That thirty pounds was more than enough to pay for his entry here. He could have a beer or two. He couldn't help but raid his bacon sarnies as soon as he sat down, just after eleven. He had his "Times" for the lunch and tea intervals, when others would be festively conversing in the marquees.

He remembered a story told by a cricket commentator, the late Brian Johnston, about an incident at this ground. The butler had been umpiring, when his Duke was clearly run out. What was he to do? Would giving out his Master be a sackable act of treason? He had simply declared, solemn facedly: "His Grace is not in!"

Runs flowed freely, as the home county's bowlers wilted under the early after-noon's sun; it was great weather for the start of September. No one seemed to mind the carnage. There were more important things in life: beauty of setting; beauty of panama and blazer, of parasol and floating dress; beauty of friendship and conviviality. With slight bitterness for a moment, Matthew reflected on the ugliness that he now faced.

He dozed. The sun and the second beer had done their tricks. The gaudily decorated deck-chair sagged under-neath him.

"Good heavens, if it isn't Matt." Matthew stirred, confusedly.

"Matt: how are you?". Putting back on his glasses, which had slipped onto his stomach, Matthew squinted. Who was this? It was Olly.

Matt and Olly had known each other at University, along with Robert and Johnny. Matthew had styled himself in those days as Matt, given that it had sounded no nonsense. He'd redesignated himself as Matthew once Ordination had approached. Sadly, they'd not kept in touch.

"Are you Olly? Is that right?" Matthew decided to stick to the old name, redolent as it was of happier times. Whether Olly had become Oliver, he didn't enquire. Olly was a jolly, flowing, and now very popular name.

"Yes, Matt. Dead right."

"Well, what are you doing, Olly?"

"Let's have a drink, Matt, and I'll tell you. Come into the marquee. I'm a member." It was just before Tea.

Matthew was rather glad that he'd come by bus and train, as the champagne corks popped. The canapes were delicious. Suddenly, he realised that he had left behind his bacon butties, but then the sea-gulls would be worthy recipients.

Everyone was joshing, but not jostling. They seemed pleased to be introduced to Olly's friend. Any friend of his was a friend of theirs. There was none of that looking over the shoulder, for another more interesting person to talk to, that often you had over Coffee before Church Meetings.

"Well, what have you been doing Matt?"

"Oh, drifted into School-teaching, then turned my collar around."

64

Reminiscing, they roared with laughter. Matthew hadn't laughed so heartily since, along with Robert and Johnny, they'd once climbed onto the roof of one of the most venerable Chapels at Oxford. He had come to wish that he could still laugh raucously. Something had died within himself.

For him, Ordination, first as a Deacon and then as a priest, was a death and a new life. St Paul had written that to be a Christian was to become a new creation. At his Ordination as a priest, he had had to walk up to a kneeling stool, bending his neck before the bishop, as maybe ten or fifteen priests, in praying, had formed a holy scrum of outstretched arms over him. It had been pitch dark, before the light of emerging into priestly Ordination. Even at that moment, Matthew's mind had gone back to that moment in Masonic Initiation when the blindfold had been ripped away.

At Theological College, the buzz had been portentously of the "Ontological Change" through Ordination, a change in being.

During his thirty odd years of being Ordained, he had become gradually a bit different. At one level, he was still the same awkward School-boy. Maybe, he reflected, all adults are updates on their childhood selves. Yet, he had come to know a priest's need to hold back in conversation, and to take verbal hammer blows. Maybe, that's why the pipe, and the glass of scotch, were such good silent friends.

He'd become, though, the man who had hit Sarah, in his rage. He'd done violence to himself through pills.

For now, Matthew was able to hoot in laughter. He knew Church members who liked to be seen to perch as wise old owls. He suspected that, viewing him, they hooted to each other only in derision

"Come to my Club, Matt, next week. You and I can have a quiet chat."

Waking from that pleasant dream, Matthew resolved that he must meet up with Olly, and perhaps Robert and Johnny.

Johnny gave him Olly's 'phone number. A lunch-time date at the Club was arranged. "Good heavens, if it isn't Matt", Olly had replied on the 'phone.

Robert and Johnny couldn't make it, but it would be fun to see Olly again, and no doubt all four of them could soon meet up together.

Matthew now researched, with anticipation, the best times and prices for a trip to Town.

Chapter 13
The Club

"Yes, I ought to go in a dog collar," Matthew thought to himself. He'd worn a casual shirt in that dreamed match up on the Downs. Here, though, was a sign of his clerical position, albeit not proof, as anyone could order online a black shirt and collar. It took some queenish self-confidence, though, for an impostor to enter a shop of ecclesiastical fitters.

At his Theological College, the rule had been, in terms of wearing black: never before Ordination, always after-wards. As for unorthodoy in sexual morality, it was prudent for some ambitious Clerics to reverse that sequence.

Ordinands never swanned around his Theological College in black. Presumption, though, lay in addressing each other, when walking past, as "Father".

Some Ordinands used to froth that they "couldn't wait to Get into Black".

One of his training Vicars claimed to be able to tell, from a Cleric's shirt colour and type of Clerical collar, the vintage: which Theological College, and, more precisely, the decade. Matthew always wore black, with a small inset collar: sometimes, and pleasingly, he was taken for a Roman Catholic. He couldn't comprehend how some Clergy went through a day, especially in sweaty necky summer, with those all-round rings of confidence, so heavily studded.

Clerical life for Matthew would often involve several changes of clothing a day, especially in the summer: black for work; light coloured casuals, even with shorts, for padding around the Vicarage; scruffy for hacking brambles in his always unwieldy garden.

Having now brushed his black suit, he buffed up his shoes, just in time, runningly, to catch the bus. Clubland meant it was best not to drive even to the local station. He'd been to Masonic Dinners in the Clublands. You paid a lot (say £60.00), but it was all inclusive. As they said in "Benidorm": the temptation was to "fill your boots!" Small sips were best, as the most vigilant of waiters would always top up. Probably, as the tradition went, they would have poured wine through your fingers if you had tried to cover up the glass.

Sitting down in the train, he looked across at and recognised a benign looking passenger. A few years' before Matthew, he'd been to the same Preparatory School in Shropshire. This actor was best known for playing a vet who had to put his arm up animals unmentionably. Matthew had once asked him to open the Church Fayre, but he had been away on tour.

Matthew introduced himself accordingly. Without a touch of arrogance, his newly found companion chatted with him, of escapades and characters at School long ago, when each of them had worn caps and blazers.

As they bid each other good-bye at Victoria, Matthew wondered which television or film studio the other was heading for.

Matthew loved the walk to St James'. He'd done it many times, often to and from Masonic Meetings. It was always a thrill and, he felt, a privilege to walk past Buck. Palace, and especially on the return as it was flood-lit. Having traversed Green Park, he strolled past "The Ritz". He remembered that evening when, going to a Masonic Meeting, he had just missed seeing the flashing lights as the then Prince of Wales and Mrs Parker-Bowlers had made their first, and rehabilitating, public appearance.

Flags floated in the breeze, as Matthew walked up the slightly daunting steps of the ancient Universities' Club. It was always a little intimidating entering such hallowed precincts, but, once the Porter was satisfied as to propriety of dress, and of attitude, with a quick word as to purpose, all was well.

He'd been there for Masonic Dinners, fine all inclusive ones, and also to dine with Johnny, on several occasions. He knew that the cloak-room had pegs with chains and their locks. You slid the chain down the inside of the sleeve of a coat, and then up the outside, locking its' chain on a hook at the top, trying not to lose the key in the coming hours.

The reading rooms were agreeably sepulchral. The bar was always jolly, with in winter a warming fire. The dining-room was a place in which to have duck pate, roast lamb, and then English cheeses. There was space for private conversation. Living on the coast and thus unable to visit often, Matthew couldn't justify membership (given the expense) but he sometimes hankered after it.

"It is good to see you, Matt", Olly warmly greeted Matthew, as by arrangement, he entered the bar. "What will you have?". Such was a place for a "Bloody Mary, please."

In the bar and over duck pate, and roast lamb, they swapped stories and memories of Oxford days, of holidays, and of friendships either lost or won. They chortled over that time when they'd all go up on the roof.

The Club Claret was suitably mellowing.

Matthew told Olly something of his life as a priest. As he did so, he noticed a slight sadness in Olly's eyes.

"I was a priest, too, Matt."

Matt was staggered.

"What do you mean,Olly? I thought you'd always been a stock-broker."

Olly hesitated, diverting himself in sipping the excellent Club Port, and slicing portions of the English cheeses.

Matthew knew that this was a time for silence. As a priest, you had to be unembarrassed enough to allow for a silence within which, hesitatingly, the other person had a chance to start articulating a profound truth about him or her self.

Olly went on to tell his tale. He'd gone from Oxford to the City. He had enjoyed stock-broking, yet there had been an inner pain (Matthew had known it, too): he knew that he had to be Ordained. His hope was to be both a stock-broker and a priest: to serve honourably both God and Mammon. He would be a Christian presence in the City. He'd undergone the training, by evening and week-end, somehow fitting it all in. Not for him those Ordinands' sherry parties before Evensong.

Ordained deacon and then priest, he had served at the Church of a Livery Company. Negatively put, he had been a "Non Stipendiary Minister". These days, the term was "Self Supporting Minister". To Matthew, even that term failed: isn't it God who supports us?

Word had got through, though, to Olly's Diocese that he was a practising homosexual. Not a formal Complaint, but a whisper of, as euphemistically out, "concern".

For decades, two subjects (amongst a limited list of others) had transfixed the Church of England: what people do in bed; what some do in Lodge.

The Church of England had come, generously, to accept that homosexual men and women were not evil by nature, although perhaps some of the more zealous of the Evangelicals might have fantasised about getting out the brush-wood for a good day's burning. Generally, Orientation was considered to be okay- thus exculpating many great figures and heroes, even, unbelievably, some Evangelical ones.

Homosexual Practice by Laity had come to be seen as just about fair enough, if there was fidelity. Practice by Clergy was another matter altogether. An example had to be set by Clergy, who thus seemingly had a higher Calling than the Laity. Implicitly, it seemed, tolerance of Lay Practice was thereby shown to be hollow.

For Clergy, homosexual cohabitation was okay. Going to homosexual Clubs was okay. Hugging and touching were okay. Civil partnerships were okay (but not marriages).

All, so long as there wasn't anything done genitally.

To Matthew, it seemed rather prurient and unnecessary. Surely, loving fidelity was all. He wasn't gay himself. In some ways he was too emotionally retarded for any sexual relationship, but he had known many gays. At Theological College, even some marrieds had had other such diversions, cruelly so (as it seemed to Matthew) to their wives.

Also, unless cameras were placed in every Vicarage's bed-room, or indeed any other room, how could it all be policed?

Still, the Church held, especially regarding its' Princes, to the saving difference between Orientation and Practice, or rather seeming Practice. Tale was told of a now married and very highly placed Prince who'd been thus photographed in bed with a fellow Ordinand. The photographer had proudly kept the snap.

It appeared to Matthew that often those condemning the most vehemently were the ones most at war with something in themselves that they feared and despised, but with which they were, perhaps, inescapably fascinated.

"What happened, Olly?"

"They told me to be more discreet. My partner and I agreed not to visit each other. We kept it to holidays. Mind you, he was already rather busy running his Diocese."

"What, you mean, he was a Bishop?"

71

"Yes, in the west country, one of the ones who used to condemn the gays."

As a second glass of port was enjoyed, Olly carried on to speak of a time of stability and yet of necessary subterfuge, until another arrow had been fired. A formal Complaint alleged that Olly was a City Freemason (which he was), but supposedly appointed by the Freemasons to infiltrate the part of the Diocese where the City lay.

The Complainant had been a closet, practising, homosexual Archdeacon, who was perhaps terrified of a leak by the well informed Olly. He was eagle nosed, and indeed had talons.

Nauseated by the hypocrisies of the Church and yet grieved, Olly had relinquished his working Ministry as a priest. In the City, he could try to be a Christian in his principles, and privately to offer priestly counsel and comfort. Olly was ebullient, as ever, but his eyes remained sad.

One more port wouldn't do any harm. Matthew told his own tale about being a Masonic Cleric, and then asked for advice. Olly hesitated. Genuinely and not piously, he replied; "Pray about it. Just pray about it. Even I still pray sometimes".

Maybe, some quiet and uninsistent prayer might help. Possibly, Matthew ought even to go on a Retreat.

At the entrance, he bid Olly a fond good-bye. Olly seemed relieved to have told his tale. Effervescently, Olly went into the bar, for a drink with his stock-broking friends. Matthew thought that his own stock price was falling,

Its' being still summer Matthew had no over-coat to unlock and unchain. Whether he liked it or not, he might be freed soon from his own locks and chains.

Chapter 14
The Temple

Early on that morning, in mid September, as the train had gone through the fields of West Sussex, Matthew had wondered gloomily whether, like the gently grazing sheep and cows in their pastures, he would one day be slaughtered. He'd gently grazed in Parishes, but now feared the Church's knife.

Since seeing Olly, he had spent some days at the Vicarage brooding on Olly's words and experience. Parish and School life had continued in its COVID pattern. Yes, for Harvest, he had managed to find a Speaker from "Air Ambulance". COVID meant Church couldn't host the 5 and 6 year olds with their Seasonal singing about "Cauliflowers fluffy". There was talk of a second Lock-down, or at least a "circuit-breaker" at half-term.

He had come to conclude that he must take advice from the High Priests of Freemasonry. So, here he was, returning to Town. At least, he would receive brotherly love there.

Owlishly and benevolently, the high ranking official of the Secretariat beamed over his half-rimmed glasses at Matthew, in an office where Matthew noticed that there was a decanter of whisky. Coffee, though, had been offered by a secretary on his arrival in the ante-room; Noon hadn't quite yet been reached.

HQ was a magnificent Art Deco building in Holborn. Its' main Temples were gorgeously, and in some cases Orientally, ornamented.

Some of its' more bellicose opponents took, and indeed celebrated, it as proof of decadent paganism.

The corridors were wide and well polished, and the main stair-case sweeping. It was no wonder that it had been a location for "Spooks", and cat-walks of fashion shows. For Matthew, in his bitterest moments, the Church seemed to work in shadows, and to be self-preening.

"Well, Matthew, good to see you again. Sit down, please."

Matthew settled himself down.

"We did try to talk to the Church a few years' ago. I think it was in a Diocese just next to yours. Somebody had been kicking up a stink about Masons' supposedly running everything there. We met the Cathedral's Dean. He seemed a bit uncomfortable. He'd been, and we knew of course, Provincial Grand Lodge Chaplain up in the Midlands. He'd given it all up- maybe he'd been advised that it wasn't, so to speak, good for his career. Politely, he told us just to drop the whole matter, not to respond. Not to rock the boat. So, we left it. It's only going to get worse for you, I'm afraid."

"Well, what do you suggest?", Matthew asked worriedly.

"I don't know. I'm so sorry. I hate to say it, but you could have just to resign, either from the Church or else from the Craft. There's plenty that we could ask you to do."

Matthew thanked his kind host. Spirits' low, he nevertheless found, as ever, a slight spring in his step as he walked along the Temple's grand corridors, and down its' winding stair-case. No doubt others had walked those elegant paths with anxieties oppressing them.

Returning home, in mid after-noon, he noticed once more the sheep and cows' grazing away, as ever seemingly unworried. Perhaps, as animals, they couldn't foresee their own futures.

Chapter 15
The Parochial Church Council

At the turn of September, Harvest had been judged a great success: inventive displays of flowers; a fine Speech by the Air Ambulance, justly rewarded by generous donations; the Congregation enjoying humming along to the hymns.

As at Christmas, certain hymns had to be at Harvest, almost by force of holy extortion on the vicar. There had been a near riot in his first Parish at the omission of "We plough the fields and scatter", albeit there hadn't been many fields for scattering in that part of suburbia. Matthew liked it when, on leaving the Service on a wet Harvest Sunday morning, people would mumblingly grumble about the weather, having rejoiced in song over the "soft refreshing rain".

There was a cycle, reassuring in a way, from Harvest through All Souls', to Remembrance Sunday, Advent and Christmas, and on to Lent, Holy Week, and Easter, and finally the Festivals of late Spring (Trinity with its' mystery, and Corpus Christi with its' exoticism). Come mid to late June, there was a chance to draw breath. To adapt it, "Sell in May, and go away", as stock-brokers like Olly might say. That rhythm gave shape, as in the life of a School-master, to the ordinary turning of month to month.

Interpolated were business Meetings, and administrative requirements. The Parochial Church Council met next in early October. Matthew had drawn up a purposeful, but, he trusted, anodyne Agenda. It was right both to review the continuing arrangements for COVID, and also to consider initiatives for when it was all over. Plans for Advent and Christmas had to be finalised. Hall hire fees for the next year needed to be set. A Faculty was required for repairing the leaking roof.

Gone was the summer heat and twilight of the previous Meeting. For several months now, Meetings would have to be in electrically lit rooms with drawn curtains, and, God willing, the boiler's working. Matthew wished that, as in business, Meetings could be at 11.00 a.m. or 2.30 p.m., when the mind was sharp, and people had other things to go on to.

Two minutes before the start, he noticed "Just checking" creep in, nodding to a couple of members of the Council; they nodded back. People who were not members of the Church Council were always welcome, and Matthew would encourage them to speak if they wished to. Recalling that time of "Just Praying", Matthew tried to block this man out of his mind. He knew that there was going to be trouble. Why had the man nodded to those two members? He wished that he had had a Scotch before-hand.

All proceeded smoothly, if rather lengthily, as some members enjoyed vocally having a good night out's worth. Then came the notorious "Any Other Business". Some clergy would boast that, craftily, they always kept the most contentious item to Any Other Business. It didn't forewarn opponents. By that stage, usually nearly two hours in, most members were tired, and, in some cases, in fear of the wrath of a beloved one for being allegedly late home. Difficult issues could be waved through.

Lay opponents of a vicar would use A.O.B. to raise a new hum-dinger, the Vicar's having had no chance to research, to think, and, if absolutely necessary, to pray about it.

Matthew had devised a procedure whereby members were requested to submit any items for A.O.B. at least forty eight hours' in advance, along with any supporting papers. However, by the Church of England's law, if three quarters of the members present at the Meeting consented, the unannounced item could be considered, albeit most members wanted to keep to the two hours' unofficial minimum and maximum timing. It was amazing that, respectively, matters could be protracted and accelerated accordingly.

"I've had a chat with a couple of your members, Father", he began. Matthew always distrusted people who would sometimes, opportunistically, drop their habitual addressing of him by his first name.

"Just Checking" wanted to say a few words. He had heard that visitors were welcome to come to speak, and even to speak the truth in love. Matthew caught a glimpse of one of the nodders' fiddling in a coat-pocket; was he audio recording the Meeting?

In the name of the Holy Grails of Openness, Transparency, and Accountability, Matthew said, with as sincere a smile as he could muster, that he was sure that everyone would be pleased to hear from him. He suspected correctly that the subject was his own Freemasonry, and also that the power and influence of the two nodders would win if Matthew tried to defer it all by putting it to a vote on that three quarters threshold. Maybe, too, hounds (in addition to the nodders) scented now the blood of a good chase.

"Just Checking" finished his Speech, as sluggishly the clock ticked well into the second quarter of the third hour. Entirely predictably to Matthew, he had raided the Bible for selective quotations; he had raised high a copy at one stage. Here had been, as before, sentimentality and paranoia. He had climaxed it in an undefined, and yet heroic, cry for God's Mission for His Church to be honoured. He had said it all standing. He had sat down sweating.

Matthew could but bluster.

"Well, thank you for sharing your thoughts. I didn't know that this subject would be raised."

He paused, and then steeled himself: "I can answer all your points, but it is now too late in the evening."

A loyalist added: "Can't we just leave it for another time? Father Matthew said that he hadn't known about its' being brought up tonight. I hadn't. It's getting late."

The members agreed. Perhaps they were weary at this very late stage of the Meeting. Matthew couldn't tell their thoughts. No one had dismissed the claims as preposterous, yet, as they left the Hall, worryingly they were talking animatedly amongst themselves. Matthew could not but over-hear the nodders inviting "Just Checking" to the pub.

As he had forecast to himself before getting back to the Vicarage, Matthew had to rely through the night on the BBC World Service.

Chapter 16
On and In Retreat

Things had become so bad that Matthew had no option other than to go on a Retreat. For years, he had justified to himself his not doing so- too busy in the parish; no Clergy cover. Now, though, he needed time to think and maybe even pray, though he knew that it would be painful.

Being earlyish October, it was a shade too soon for the Retreat's to be diverted to Christmas cards. He ensured that he had the essentials: his Morning and Evening Prayer; paper for jotting down ruminations; baccy; a bottle of scotch.

He had been to this place in Kent just before Ordination. It was a tradition of his Theological College that the Retreats run by Dioceses immediately before Ordination as a Deacon could not be guaranteed to be "sound". So, just in case, a proper one ought to be arranged before-hand for the College's Ordinands.

A Steward of the Retreat House once told Matthew of one well-built Ordinand who, on arrival, had walked up the Drive, holding, sweatily and unashamedly, a portable television, and a six pack. Probably, the rest of his booze had been in his suit-case. The Steward had confiscated what he could see, along with the telly.

The Retreat House was set in glorious wood-lands.

Matthew had almost forty eight hours booked in. That was a very long time.

His last Sunday Service had ended by Noon, and the next Mass wasn't until early on the Wednesday. He would leave by late Tuesday after-noon.

Sunday's Supper at 7.00 p.m. of macaroni cheese was fine. There was one other Retreatant. Protocol had to be observed of silently gesturing for the salt and pepper, or for the water. The bowls for the fruit salad's having been cleared away by 7.30 p.m., Matthew didn't know what to do next. It was a bit early to go to bed. He strolled around the gardens, until it became chilly, and then the Library, whose stoutly bound, and no doubt worthy, tomes of Theology failed to seduce him.

Matthew poured a scotch, lay on his bed, and thought. His intention to resolve his future became side-tracked by memories of Sarah. He knew it would happen, especially if he came on Retreat, which could only be but self-indicting.

In the New Town, he'd met Sarah, a bubbly nurse, whilst visiting someone in the local Hospital. Somehow it just happened. They went out for drinks, walks, and meals. She'd had had some experience of Church, back in her native East Anglia. She came to Worship. She came to the Church Summer's Fete. She came to the Harvest Supper. Sarah had survived the places where dragons roamed. She was liked.

Soon they were married. The Bishop had Officiated for them in their Church.

For several years, Matthew had requested, politely he hoped, the main participants of a Wedding not to be late. It wasn't always possible. Matthew got to the Church for his Wedding with two minutes to spare. The Bishop was ten minutes' late; a railway-crossing had been uncooperative. Sarah was fifteen minutes' late, but then a Noon start is always a tight call for a bride.

Admittedly, the Bishop had already been purportedly welcomed at about 11.30 a.m. A Clerical friend (the Vicar of a Parish very near to the Houses of Parliament) had arrived in a frock coat, sartorially honouring Sarah and Matthew. The altar servers had warmly greeted him, for garbed thus he could only be but the Bishop. Having escorted him into the Vestry, they had then enquired whether either they could fetch his vestments from his car, or he'd like to use the Church's robes in the Vestry cup-board. He'd had to reveal his identity, to gracious laughter all round.

The Bishop displayed, for a bachelor, remarkable insight in his sermon. He had great stamina through that hot day's hour and a half of Nuptial Mass. The sun shone as they received their guests at the local Sports' Club.

It was hard to keep track. Some people from the Service were now missing. Others were now at the Club unexpectedly. It didn't matter too much.

By early evening, Matthew and Sarah were off for Italy. Matthew had insisted, maybe over much, that there not be the delay of an evening party. Anyway, he wasn't a good dancer, at least not in front of parishioners.

Honeymooning on an Italian island had been golden. The Bay of Naples was stunning by day and by night. The only thing was that ladies had to be careful when boat-men took them into the famous local grotto. Matthew and Sarah heard of two tales.

Matthew (37) and Sarah (33) had settled into, for each of them, their first married life. She continued to be a nurse. He enjoyed referring to her as "my wife", albeit he would immediately and wincingly realise his fault of sounding proprietorial

Matthew's problem was his emotional immaturity. He could give to parishioners pastorally, but he could not give of himself in the closest possible relationship. He couldn't give enough, emotionally or sexually. As an only child, had he been too close to his mother? Or, had he become just too set in his ways?

But then, a year in, that man had spoken to her in the Parish's local pub at the bar. She'd gone up to get some pork scratchings. Matthew knew him. He went to another Church near-by. Censoriously, Matthew considered him to be a lech.

They seemed to Matthew to be flirting. His insecurity about himself, emotionally and sexually, was ignited.

"Sarah, we're going", he whispered, as she came back with the pork scratchings. Being a Priest, he knew not to create a scene.

"We've only just arrived, Matt." Up till now, he'd always liked her calling him that.

" No. We're going. Don't make a scene."

Matthew guided her arm with covert firmness as they left.

"Good to see you, Father. Early Service tomorrow? Bye Sarah", the innocent parishioner bade them.

The Vicarage was just over the road. They stood in the living-room. The curtains were closed.

"What the hell were you doing, Sarah?"

"Just getting some scratchings."

"You flirted with him."

"Don't be ridiculous. You're paranoid because you're no damn good at it."

Matthew's right hand broke her nose. Bleeding, she called the ambulance.

"That looks bad, love. What happened?"

" Fell down the stairs."

Noticing Matthew's sheepishness, the paramedic continued:

"Are you sure that was all?"

"Yes, thanks. Just get me to the hospital, please."

Sarah's mother had taken her away, straight after the surgery. The divorce had been publicly and nobly finessed by her as due to "irreconcilable differences". Matthew had become one of those Clerics, once despised by himself, who were secret wife-beaters.

Such ghosts came back to Matthew, but he found that a second scotch enabled him, if fittingly, to get some sleep in mid evening.

By 3.30 a.m. (a cruel hour, at the best of times), he was awake. He made himself a cup of tea from the sachets on his tray, biting into a Rich Tea biscuit.

What he'd done to Sarah had been unforgivable. He'd been lucky not to face charges. What to do now, though? He resorted to prayer. It even went on for half an hour. No divine answer came. He snoozed.

Poached eggs on toast were for break-fast. Pity that there was no daily newspaper. Matthew would escape the holy precincts, and buy one. Returning from the local shop, he dropped off his 'paper in his room, and went off for a walk, past a golf-course that was almost enigmatically tucked away at the bottom of a hill. On his several Retreats here, he'd never seen anyone playing there.

Once back at the Retreat House, his mind was forming. He trusted that what was emerging might be God's idea, too. Perhaps, he ought to resign as a Church of England Cleric, and make his own way in life. He enjoyed the steak and kidney pudding for lunch, and the fruit crumble. On that Monday mid afternoon, he apologised to the Steward for having to leave a day early, and then paid his full fees. He said that he had urgent matters to attend to. The quiet and wise Steward's face suggested that he knew that Retreats often bring clarity.

Matthew drove off. This Covid Cleric, this Masonic Cleric, was now to be a Retiring Cleric.

Locking his car on the Vicarage's Drive in late after-noon, he looked up to his high roof and chimney. Usually, there were at least one or two birds perching there at this time of day. They had all flown. Maybe it was only that it was Autumn. Maybe, too, though, birds were just canny.

PART THREE:

A RETIRING CLERIC

Chapter 1

"But soon you will find that there comes a time For making your mind up."

As he tried to sleep, Matthew's mind went to his very early twenties, when Britain's zesty song had won "The Eurovision Song Contest". Their gimmick had been to rip off outer garments just as the song had begun. Matthew felt that, emotionally, he was being de-layered. His Bucks' Fizz had gone flat. Such was at the level of feeling. Now, he needed thought. He needed to make his mind up.

On the Tuesday morning, he resolved to spend time writing down the pros and cons, and then to decide between them.

PROS:

(1) He wouldn't have to get up at 5.30 a.m. every Sunday.

(2) He could have a full night's sleep, and then a lie-in, through Christmas Eve and into the Great Morning.

(3) He would no longer be receiving pay to be "nice". Vicars were paid neither to lose their temper, nor to answer back, nor forcefully to contradict someone: and especially not with swear-words.

(4) He wouldn't have to be at the mercy of people's pulling him in different directions. It was presumptuous, and arguably blasphemous, to put it on the same scale as Christ's being stretched on the Cross, but it didn't half hurt.

(5) He wouldn't have occasionally to bite his tongue at Meetings, as insults and false accusations speared in on him, his shield's being that of only a silent, slightly pained, smile.

CONS:

(1) He had a stable way of life. The Church's Year had its' pattern of Services and School Assemblies, albeit disrupted of late by COVID. What was more, once a Service or Assembly had got going, his nerves usually simmered down a little, so that he could enjoy it to some degree.

(2) He had the round of other different Services and Duties, but freedom to do things off the cuff.

(3) He had a large, free house, and also an income at just about the national average.

(4) Even the difficult characters usually at least meant well.

(5) He enjoyed talking to anyone about anything in the street, and felt chuffed when they called him "Father", "Vicar", or even "Vic".

(6) It was a privilege when, on the street, or in private, someone opened up to him something of the heart. It was an honour to be asked to keep a confidence. Matthew knew that he had his faults, but he was not, at least he hoped he wasn't, a gossipy Cleric.

Such were just a few of his ruminations, over his pipe. He coughed a little. He ought to cut down, but couldn't at the moment.

He thought that prayer for guidance might be necessary. For him, he saw this type of praying (as with praying for others) as a distilling, or purifying, of the mind. Neither type of praying was properly about sending up an arrow prayer. Neither of them was a desperate request for help, fired up to the Deity, with a reply's being supposedly dispatched, as if by Special Delivery's return of post. Rather, the purpose of each was to try to filter out selfish motives and consequently to prompt the right action.

Human nature seemed to him to have an innate selfishness. Maybe, the need to survive, physically, was at its' root. For Matthew, pure selflessness in a human being lay only in Christ, and in his self-offering on the Cross. For that work, Christ was unique, and could and indeed ought to be worshipped as divine.

Matthew found arguments that Christ had taken our punishment on the Cross to be simplistic. "Penal substitution", Christ's paying our due penalty, seemed to have sometimes, wittingly or not, an unhealthy interest in punishment. Christ's work had been first and foremost one of self-giving love.

By the gentle power of the Holy Spirit, it seemed to Matthew that a human being could begin the process of becoming less selfish. Although such a pursuit was for a Christian an attempt (albeit falteringly given human fallibility) to imitate Christ's self offering, it seemed to him to be arrogance to claim such as an exclusively Christian spiritual exercise. He resisted, though, the unintentionally patronising idea of "anonymous Christians": someone's being a Christian without his or her realising it. That was an attraction to him of Freemasonry, with its' stress on developing (with God's help) one's own faith, whilst having due hesitancy and timidity in trying to judge the souls of others.

Through the process for him now of praying for guidance, he made up his mind that he had to go. Often, he struggled to make up his mind. Now, he had perceived that selfishness lay not only in clinging on to his stable and material advantages, but also in not accepting that his Ministry had grown stale. The people of the Church and Parish needed a young lion. He could continue to chat to people in the street, or elsewhere, about their hopes and fears, their joys and sorrows, their successes and their regrets, their deeds of noble spirit and their unresolved guilts.

He'd made up his mind. He sensed in himself some relief, and, strangely, a little Fizz.

Chapter 2
Resignation

Matthew's letter had to be one of both resignation, and also of a retirement that was some six or seven years' early. He wrote it a couple of days later, as he had wanted to be sure in his mind, and also to check his finances. They were okay, but not fantastic. He wouldn't have enough to buy a house outright, and might even struggle to put down a deposit. However, he could rent a one-bedroomed flat for a while.

Until relatively recently, most retired Clergy could earn a fair increment from Funerals, and also, in doing so, feel pastorally self-fulfilled. Now, Funerals were scarce for Clergy, whether retired or even still in post. It seemed that most Funerals were now taken by non religious Celebrants.

In his early days, it was taken as read that the local Vicar, or (deputisingly) the Curate, would be asked to take the vast majority of Funerals. Not a few Clerics had moaned then that they spent most of their time taking Funerals (usually, and loudly, bewailing the fact that the fees went only to the Diocese). Nowadays, many hectored away about their lack of Funerals, with seemingly their having a sense that they had become spiritually side-lined. The Dioceses had noticed the plummet in income.

Some commentators said that it was all a sign of the nation's becoming more secular. Not a few of the Biblically fire-breathing Clerics contended, however, that it all came from people's growing spiritual cowardice when challenged by the Gospel's message of sin, with its' choice between repentance or hell-fire. For them, paradoxically, such Proclamation of Fire had to be redoubled.

Either way, Matthew knew that Clerics had often been reluctant to take on "yet another" funeral, or had been awkward about arrangements, or had simply for days not replied to answer-phone requests from Under-takers, who had at hand bereaved families understandably anxious to make arrangements swiftly.

Matthew would make himself available, in retirement, to take a Funeral, but a goodly source of income could not be guaranteed. Even his thinking now along those in part slightly mercenary lines made him feel uncomfortable with himself. After over three decades, he'd probably have to find a job again.

The letter to the Bishop contained all the legal necessities. It was short. It gave no reasons; it didn't have to. The Bishop's reply was prompt. It was courteous. No problems, Masonic or otherwise, were alluded to. He wished Matthew well, and would pray for him.

Within a week it had all been done. Matthew recalled the sense of execution at his Ordination as a priest, and then consequently of new life. Here again was an execution, by force of circumstance, but not especially a feeling of new life. Although not feeling bitter, Matthew once more felt that his Fizz had gone flat.

By Church law, he had three remaining months of Service as Vicar, and then three months to vacate the Vicarage. He would announce his resignation on the following Sunday. Being mid October it meant that he would have a final Christmas there.There was talk of another lock-down, though, in November. How would Christmas be?

His last Sunday would be in mid January. He hoped that it would be a bright winter's day, with some snow-drops' at least peeping through the turf in the Church-yard. He had to be out of the Vicarage by mid

April. Easter was early in April. He would say a private Mass of Easter, in the Vicarage. He would burn incense and say many times "Alleluia!" He hoped that he would be able to rejoice that the strife was over, and the battle done.

Resignation, and especially retirement, couldn't just be announced with the Notices at the start of a Service, but had to be at the end. Otherwise, throughout the Service, minds could not help but be distracted, whether confused, perturbed, or delighted. Feeling slightly low at heart, he would conduct the two Services as professionally as possible,

As the small group of worshippers left the early Service, they agreed with him that they would not send this piece of intelligence viral. At the end of the later Service, a member of the local Praetorian Guard gave public words of thanks, and applause rang out. A couple of people nodded to each other.

Good wishes and thanks were sincere as people left the Church; Matthew's spirits lifted a little. Perhaps, though, it was helpful that COVID meant no Coffee, and thus no lingering and prolonging

Later, on walking home and past the local pub, Matthew noticed the two nodders going in with "Just Checking", no doubt to uncork the Fizz.

Chapter 3
Good Toast

From experience, Matthew knew that, once you had announced your departure, proverbially you were toast. It was improper for the Cleric to attempt any longer to steer the Church's policies. There was no point now in a lay-person's trying to win the Cleric's favour, maybe in hope of getting that particular job or role at Church; such would have to wait until the arrival of the next Cleric. Such was a huge relief to Matthew.

Anything that was remotely contentious, or required months of detailed work, could be heftily and safely kicked, as if it were a rugby ball, straight into the higher parts of one of the Stands. The trick was not to sound too lofty, or pleased, when saying once again:

"Well, I really must leave it to my successor."

He liked to think of it as being like Good Toast. As a truism, most people like Good Toast. Burnt Toast is the problem. As it disappears down the mouth and throat, Good Toast can be savoured, with its' oozing butter and delicious spread. Bad Toast is usually chucked into a bin, or for the birds. As long as the departing Cleric continues to do the required Services and other duties, remains nice, doesn't complain nor try to fix the future of the parish, he or she is bound to be cherished as a slice of Good Toast: disappearing, yet relished. He would endeavour to be Good Toast.

There was no need to listen to BBC World Service after the few remaining Meetings of the Church Council. In any case, November's latest lock-down meant that, antiseptically, for a while Meetings were by ZOOM.

Matthew could simply turn up for the Services on his own. He kept his circular letters and his 'phone calls going.

The workers at the Amenity Tip were friendly and helpful, guiding him as to which skip to use. COVID meant that one of them hadn't been able to visit his family in Eastern Europe for a whole year. It was quietest and thus best to go when there was rain fore-cast.

Twenty years of goods at the Vicarage made for many journeys. He shredded those parish documents which he trusted weren't essential, and piled others into the Church Hall, along with every artefact from the Vicarage that he knew wasn't his. He didn't want to be accused of either negligence or theft.

Going through papers was time consuming. Issues came to mind, happy days were evoked by photographs, and memories of departed ones were stirred.

Able to plan their retirements well in advance, most clergy clear papers in a more leisurely way, say good-bye gradually to local people and groups, attend Retirement Courses (preparing their minds and finances), and especially settle on future housing.

The rental agencies were friendly and diligent, but:

"The market's a bit slack, Sir, for what you are looking at, especially given this Lock-down."

He wanted to stay by the sea-side. He wanted to remain living in this Parish. As he liked to try to joke to people, the fresh sea air was good for his be-smoked lungs, and the flat surfaces for his knees. He had written to the Bishop to assure him that he would neither attend the Church there, nor interfere in its' life. Folk memories were of a very long serving Vicar, of a near-by Parish, who from the moment of his retirement had sat in the front pew there, cross-armed (at least, metaphorically so).

"Should be some movement in the market early next year, Sir, once as we all hope the Lockdown's over."

Festively, and amidst national (but maybe not universal) outpourings of jubilation, there was to some degree an interlude in the Lockdown. Admittedly, Santa couldn't be invited. Carols had to be just hummed to. Matthew reflected that, even only a year previously, he had taken it all a little for granted. But, still: the Church had been open, the people had come, and he could pat himself on the back for only having had the usual three hours', or so, sleep on Christmas Night.

That would be the last of his Christmasses as a Vicar. Maybe, he'd be asked elsewhere occasionally to take a Service around about Christmas, especially when the Vicar was on a post Christmas break. As he lunched on his Christmas Day's minted sausages, and had a second dry sherry, he thought: "I'm going to miss all this." Unlike with "Carry on Cleo", and Morecambe and Wise's teasing of Des O'Connor, he would have no more Repeats.

Chapter 4
Leaving with a plastic bag

Eric Morecambe would sometimes walk off stage, wearing overalls and a cap, carrying a paper bag. Matthew remembered once seeing a previous (by then ancient) Bishop, only a few minutes' previously in the Mass all gloriously adorned in ecclesiastical vesture, return to his car carrying a mere plastic bag. It was too small to have contained those robes. Perhaps, the Chaplain had already taken them back to the car, and the Bishop wanted to stop at Tesco's on the way home.

A new Lock-down meant that in the middle of January 2001, Matthew could have no one to attend his final Sunday. As he walked into Church for the final time, he felt a pang of failure and regret, but then he looked up at the Board of Vicars' names. Yes, he had done quite a long time compared with most of them; such he trusted was not too self-congratulatory. He used to say to people, as they stood below it, that the Board was good for having lots of space under-neath his name, and that it was a salutary declaration to him that he was not the be all and end all.

Also, eventually a Vicar's name became forgotten.

"You know. The one with the glasses, who went grey. Father, what was his Name?"

Would he become: "Father, what was his name? Yes, I remember him, that, that, er, Father Malcolm."?

Here was an aide-memoire.

Usually, when Father Matthew said that no one present (looking up at the Board) would ever live the two hundred or so years that probably would be required for it to be filled with names, there had been sudden silences of intimations of mortality.

Fondly and thankfully, he thought of the past fortnight. Many people had sent him kind messages. There had been letters, texts, and e-mails. Bottles of wine (good wine) had been left on his door-step. The Treasurer had come round to present a handsome cheque from a Collection that they had secretly taken.

Each of the six hundred children of the School had drawn a picture of him, with a message to him: such was a rich reward of ministry.

The editors of two local community periodicals had interviewed him. Suspecting that they might like to photograph him, before the first interview he had had a grey hair removingly short hair-cut. The items' being published a few days before his retirement, he compared their photographs of him with one that had been in the local Paper on his relatively youthful arrival a couple of decades previously. Vainly, he was pleased and indeed surprised that there weren't now too many worry lines. He was slightly fleshier. Maybe, his ministry here hadn't been all that stressful after all. This was not the face of someone who had suffered overly.

During his final Mass, he coughed quite a lot. Perhaps, his retirement would start with one of his regular bronchitis induced periods of abstinence from the baccy.

He looked for a final time around the Church. He had come to see it as if he were its' parent. He'd never had children, but in opening the Church every morning and closing it every evening, Father Matthew had come (maybe sentimentally, but still proudly) to see it as like his child. "Time to get up." "Nighty night."

Over the years, he had done his best to look after it: to open and close the windows, to check the heating, to clear up books and papers, to pick up from the car-park the beer cans and take-away wrappers, to tidy up a storm's fallen branches in the Church-yard, and to strew salt in the snow, which was really quite boyishly enjoyable once you got going.

Father Matthew cleared his remaining items from the Vestry. He gave one final look around, as he began to sing to himself Abba's "Thank you for the music". He kissed the carpet in the porch. It wasn't the kiss of a parent at night, but of one who would never see the child again. He began to walk home, his items in a paper-bag, noticing the first slight and shy shoots of the snow-drops.

Chapter 5
Lands of lost content

Dear Reader,
If of a delicate nature, you are advised to skip this
chapter, and bits early in the next one. Maybe, if you
know anyone who, by any remote chance has read them,
you might want to ask that person kindly to give you a
sanitised resume.

Amidst the diversions of December (the exigencies of the Lockdown, of Christmas, of handling his final weeks in the Parish so that no one was offended, and of starting to find a future home), Matthew had noticed black blood. He hadn't wanted to trouble the doctors- COVID had made them busy.

The black blood had become worse over Christmas. Perhaps, it was all just stress.

A few years' previously, after red blood, endoscopies had led to a hemorrhoidectomy, with the removal also of a polyp.

Very early in January, for the first time in a long while he had made (in this case a very necessary) New Year's Resolution. He would make, as it were, a face to face appointment with a G.P. After an examination, the understandably slightly tired looking doctor still had the energy and care to say that it might just be necessary for Matthew to have an Endoscopy.

He had managed to put it off for a few days, until the Friday before he was to leave Church with his plastic bag.

He went to a part of the Hospital where he and other patients looked sheepish. Near the seats of the waiting-room, signs on the clinical doors said irrefutably: "Endoscopy". They were all in it together.

As he waited, he was glad that his mask slightly hid his smoker's cough.

As ever, the N.H.S. was good at putting Matthew at his ease. The Endoscopic technician and the nurses gave him complete confidence in them. Momentarily, Matthew wondered whether he might ever again be able to put his full trust in God.

All completed, he put on his clothes, and was then taken into a side-room. There was a poster about zero tolerance of smoking on the premises.

Hesitatingly, the Endoscopist asked Matthew whether he could wait a while for the Consultant. Matthew could. Being now on the brink of being retired, he had all the time in the world.

The Colorectal Consultant explained that, apparently, there wasn't too much to worry about, at least for the moment, but that they had taken a biopsy and would get back to him as soon as possible. They would have a few quick blood tests now, to be on the safe side.

Belatedly, on that Monday's first day of freedom, Matthew got up.

He re-read the cards, including the school childrens' cards. It had indeed all been worth it.

Half way through his baked beans on toast (a tiny amount of Marmite did the trick), he answered the 'phone. The beans could wait. The Consultant was hesitant.

"We have some news for you, Mr Wilson. Could you come in to see me, please?"

Mathew sensed that the doctor was administering one of his least pleasant duties.

"If you don't mind, I'd rather just hear it straight away, please. I don't want to wait."

"I have the results, Mr Wilson, of your Endoscopy."

"Yes?"

"Well, I am sorry to say that we found growths. As we did it, we took biopsies. There is no easy way to say it, Mr Wilson. You have cancer."

Matthew was silent, as parishioners who had had bowel cancer came too quickly to mind. "What do you suggest?"

"It's early days, but I'm afraid that it might well have gone too far for surgery, or for chemo or radio. We've looked at those blood test results. We've got some very good palliative carers, Mr Wilson."

He knew that not a few religious people have tremors of doubt as their own death toll is being rung. Matthew had heard of death-bed desertions of God.

For comfort that morning, he ate some rich Genoa Cake. Distracting himself, he thought of that time with Johnny, when they'd been on an all night train from Rome to Paris. Being a Saturday evening, Matthew had assured Johnny that such a famous line would surely have a bumper menu with fine wines, especially on a Saturday. There had been no restaurant. There had even been no buffet trolley. He and Johnny had had no water. They had known that their only fluid, vodka, would just worsen their thirst. Tooth-paste had helped. In the carriage, a man and a woman had shared together a bottle of water, eyeing Johnny and Matthew possessively. At 10.00 p.m., Johnny had offered, as the train stopped at Genoa, to make a run for it, to the hoped for cafe. The sight of apparently only semi-alive bodies on the plat-form had dissuaded him. They'd enjoyed the water at the Gare de Lyon early that Sunday morning.

By this late morning, Matthew knew that he just had to go out to talk sweet nonsenses with other people's doggies. He would like to drink water again at the Gare de Lyon, if only for the final time. He'd like to go back to Seville, and to Capri.

For this Shropshire lad, such were lands of lost content, shining plain, which he doubted that he would ever see again.

Chapter 6
Through the night of doubt and sorrow

In the course of the after-noon, Matthew Googled "terminal bowel cancer", going methodically through the check list as if shopping. It was only moderately effective in mitigating his sense of terror.

There was indeed dark red, and at other times black, blood in his stools. Constipation alternated with diarrhoea. He had noticed increasing fatigue and weakness, but had put it down to the stress of the past months. Weighing himself, he noticed that he had lost a little weight. A consolation was that he wasn't feeling sick, nor even worse was he vomiting.

Google suggested that it could all be only a matter of weeks. It could be at best a few months. He'd seen parishioners have surgery, or chemo or radio, for cancer. Sometimes, wonderfully, life had been significantly prolonged, if it had been caught early. At other times, seeing the effects of a treatment that had only slightly delayed death, he had thought that, if he ever had cancer, probably he would ask only for pain-killers. His family had no personal history of cancer, as most of them had died suddenly, of strokes, or heart-attacks. There was no close hand experience for him to draw on.

Such was now academic for Matthew now anyway, given what the Consultant had had to say. He vowed to make contact with people who'd been close to him. He would visit them, or more practically ask them to visit him. There would be a chance to say to them: thank you and farewell.

His cough was getting worse. Sometimes, he would be bent double, weepingly, trying to cough out the muck. He hadn't smoked for days.

As a distraction, he turned on "The Early Evening News". There was some disturbing story about a member of the Royal Family. COVID numbers were going up.

Matthew's cough only got worse, as self-comfortingly he watched a couple of episodes of "Dad's Army", and reflected that many of the characters played had been of an elderly age which he would not reach.

Sips of whisky didn't stop the coughing. His nightly pills usually made him sleep well. The pills helped a little this night, but nevertheless it was one of hacking coughs and thus fitful sleep. He couldn't even concentrate on the BBC World Service.

By 5.30 a.m., he had given up. At least, retired, he didn't have a Service that morning, or some other duty, at which he would have to present himself as purportedly without a trouble or illness in the world, and as fresh as a daisy. People didn't like Clerics to be troubled or ill. Was it that they didn't like self-reminders? Who could blame them?

Matthew had a box of Lateral Flow Test kits, from a scare a few months' previously. He remembered not to eat or drink anything before undergoing this ghastly, but necessary, piece of self coal-mining. As he knew he would from previously, he gagged violently. His fear of a nose bleed made him once more potentially over-cautious. Leaving the test to run its' half-hour course, he sliced meat off a chicken carcass, drank tea, and read "The

Church Times" online. There'd been another of those Clergy Discipline Cases.

"Bugger. Bugger!". The test bar was at T.

At 8.30 a.m., he 'phoned the local surgery to arrange a PCR test.

The kind Receptionist sounded concerned, reminding him to self-isolate. They'd put a kit through his letter-box at once.

Going back to bed, retching, Matthew wondered whether he'd be able now to say good-bye to people in person.

Chapter 7
"a la recherche du temps perdu";
"a snapper up of unconsidered trifles"

Rising from his mid-morning slumbers, Matthew heard a plopping sound in the porch. It was the PCR test kit. The surgery was as ever commendably, if in this case worryingly, efficient. He'd not eaten nor drunk anything for some hours, and so was eligible to do some more coal-mining. Someone in PPE would come to collect it later.

He was starting to get tetchy. That bloody cough wouldn't go away.

He thought to himself, and then regretted the implications of the term, that he would kill off some time by making lists. He had enough food and drink for now, but it was important to have a plan for the next few weeks. He'd been told that the supermarkets were good at online deliveries. He'd never done it before, but he was sure that he'd be okay. It was important to have a list of weekly domestic chores. People to 'phone, write to, e-mail, or text, needed to be listed. Little lists helped him. More precisely, the making of little lists helped him.

He didn't feel all that hungry, but there was always space for bacon sarnies, with brown sauce. Tradition demanded that he had two of them. He had the same number of glasses of very chilled dry sherry. Mentally, he'd already put those two reassuring items, familiar friends, at the top of his online list. Munching and sipping, he read yesterday's "Times" for a second time. For now, he wasn't allowed to go up to the shop for his daily paper. His father had frequently read a paper twice, starting from the front and then from the back.

Having stayed awake and enjoyed "Father Brown", he snoozed through "Morse". He'd seen that episode, like many others, several times. He liked the scenes of Oxford, many of which had been shot just before and also during the long summer vacations. He remembered once standing in the Post Office opposite Christ Church, on a sunny day near the end of the Summer Term, when excited word had got round that a road or two was being closed for filming.

Matthew realised that over the past few years he'd begun reminiscing more often, and doing so with an increasing affection. Also, of late, he'd come to grasp that (despite his Open Scholarship to Oxford, which he accepted had been achieved more by cunning than by intellect), he'd always been intellectually lazy.

There was Marcel Proust's book: "In Search of Lost Time". He'd been warned that, even in translation, it was very difficult. For that reason, Monty Python had satirised it, and he'd not read it. Matthew didn't do "difficult" books.

In his English studies, he'd been asked to read Joyce's "Ulysses", and even worse his "Finnegan's Wake." From the start, neither had offered him the faintest possibility of being in any way enjoyable. After about ten pages in the first case, and exactly two in the (to him) incomprehensible latter's, he'd given up on both of them all together. He'd resorted to short paper-back study guides to them, which somehow had just about passed muster. He'd done the same with some other authors who had simply bored him, or, for whose Essay, time had run out. Such had been Good Second stuff only, though.

He had thought that time in retirement would be gently and goldenly an invitation to think and to reminisce. Maybe, he could even write a book. His mother had always said that he ought to do so one day. Yet facing death, Matthew suspected that he would be no longer invited, but impelled, to think and to reminisce.

That after-noon, Matthew's mind went from one subject to another. Perhaps, the doses of Co Codamol that he had been taking for the wheezing were catching up on him. As he thought of his never achieved First, given two attempts, he remembered the claim that a recent Prime Minister couldn't get over the fact that a predecessor, adjacent in time to him at Oxford, had scored a First to his own Second, with his claiming that his own Second was in a far harder subject.

As for Proust and Joyce, he loved that part of an obituary of a revered Professor of Contemporary French History, from Matthew's College. That world renowned scholar of Letters was quoted as having said, airily and dismissively: "Proust and Joyce? I've heard of them. I've never read them."

It was said that that Professor would lecture, brilliantly, with a pint of beer in hand. He had been at the same Public School as Matthew.

Between their two generations, there had been, spawned from that School, many of the founding satirists of "Private Eye", with their idea from School of some people's being "Pseuds".

As Matthew understood the term, "Pseuds" tried too hard to impress; perhaps, in some not a few cases, boasting of having got through all of Proust and/or Joyce.

It seemed to Matthew that the art of not being a Pseud was to strive hard, but not to let others realise that you were doing so.

He was quite enjoying his reminiscing, when a pleasingly cheery man in P.P.E. arrived.

"Good after-noon, Sir. Just come for the PCR package. Have you done the test, Sir?"

"Oh, yes. I'll just get it?" Stupidly, he added: "Would you like to come in?"

"No, sorry, Sir, not allowed."

Returning, Matthew said with an attempted nonchalance, but slightly nervously:

"There you are. Thanks so much. I am sure that you see this sort of thing all the time. I'm not particularly worried."

The Courier hesitated, probably inadvertently. Perhaps, from experience, he knew that the rapidity of events meant that maybe Matthew had indeed got a cause to worry.

"Well, I wish you all the best, Sir."

"Thank you. Thank you!", replied Matthew, contrivedly positive.

Why had that genial Courier said "Well"?

Their conversation, and Matthew's chat with the Receptionist first thing, had been the only times that he had spoken to anyone all day.

Once upon a time, after an after-noon's pastoral visiting, he would have sometimes guiltily felt that he had simply heard too many words. He knew that many people in COVID had suffered through wordless isolation. Matthew suspected that now, to him, other people's words would without fail be welcome. In his for now constrainedly new way of life, such words would have to come only by telephone, or by letter, e-mail, or text.

He'd have to be a snapper up of otherwise unconsidered trifles. That was for now his best hope and intention. Yet, correcting himself, he reflected that no one else's other words were ever trifles.

Leaving the hallway, he went back to the kitchen, to stand and to think.

Something else was happening inside him, though. He'd known it with those moments before taking the

Zoplicone. It was the vortex. His cancer was terminally degenerative. Maybe his COVID would be deadly, too. His priesthood was a failure.

Reminiscing couldn't help Father Matthew any more. The vortex was swirling.

Chapter 8
9.40 p.m. 2021 in the Vicarage's kitchen

Matthew still had that box of Zoplicone. Why had he kept it? Had it been some sort of perverse insurance policy?

He scrambled to find it; there it was, in a kitchen drawer. Its' being swallowed, there would be no longer any vortex, but a fearful uncertainty.

In the past, a suicedee's body had not been permitted to be buried in a Church-yard.

For a priest, suicide was perhaps almost as bad as breaking the Seal of the Confessional.

Sarah, Robert, Olly, and Johnny came rapidly to mind. Matthew didn't 'phone them.

The Black Dog barked.

The kitchen's bottle of scotch no longer winked at him. The Zoplicones did.

He tried to calm himself, standing up with eyes shut and yet blinking.

Father Matthew had always preached about the survival of the soul. He'd spoken, too, of the resurrection of the body at the end of Time. God would allow believers to exist, enjoying Him forever, in their full humanity of surviving soul and, in His timing, raised body (however understood). Literally, God alone knew who were believers.

Maybe, in the sixty years or so of his earthly life, he'd done his best. Maybe not.

It seemed to him that he had failed.

He had meant well; at least he thought that he might have done.

He recalled that he'd rejoiced in publicly proclaiming God's mercy. Now, he feared God. Facing death, he agonised whether a merciful God would forgive him for fore-shortening his own life? Would God's mercy triumph over His judgement?

Perhaps, though, he thought, he didn't fear God enough.

He impatiently smoked a pipe that had grown stinkily old; coughingly, he had to stop. His hastily downed dram meant that there was still nearly a full bottle left, as salvage, for whoever might find him.

The box of Zoplicone contained enough. Feeling like a coward, he couldn't face any more of the strife and battle within himself. Such was now o'er and done, until he was to meet his Maker, whatever that might mean and entail.

At just after 9.40 p.m, in the kitchen, he died a Cancer Cleric.

He died a Masonic Cleric.

Father Matthew died a COVID Cleric.